THE TIME OF OUR LIVES

VERONICA ZUNDEL

Journeying with the Bible

THE TIME OF OUR LIVES

Published by
The Bible Reading Fellowship
First Floor, Elsfield Hall
15–17 Elsfield Way, Oxford OX2 8FG
Website: www.brf.org.uk

ISBN-10: 1 84101 441 9
ISBN-13: 978 1 84101 441 8
First published 2007
10 9 8 7 6 5 4 3 2 1 0
All rights reserved

Acknowledgments
Unless otherwise stated, scripture quotations are taken from The New Revised
Standard Version of the Bible, Anglicized Edition, copyright © 1989, 1995 by the
Division of Christian Education of the National Council of the Churches of Christ in
the USA, and are used by permission. All rights reserved.

Scripture quotations taken from the Holy Bible, New International Version, copyright
© 1973, 1978, 1984, 1995 by International Bible Society, are used by permission of
Hodder & Stoughton, a division of Hodder Headline Ltd. All rights reserved. 'NIV' is
a registered trademark of International Bible Society. UK trademark number 1448790.

Scripture quotations taken from The Revised Standard Version of the Bible, copyright
© 1946, 1952, 1971 by the Division of Christian Education of the National Council
of the Churches of Christ in the USA, are used by permission. All rights reserved.

Revised English Bible with the Apocrypha copyright © 1989 by Oxford University
Press and Cambridge University Press.

The Living Bible copyright © 1971 by Tyndale House Publishers.

The New Testament in Modern English, Revised Edition, translated by J.B. Phillips.
Published by HarperCollins Publishers Ltd.

A catalogue record for this book is available from the British Library

Printed in Singapore by Craft Print International Ltd

CONTENTS

INTRODUCTION

The Bible says it.
  I believe it.
  That settles it.

If only it were that simple! But people have disagreed for millennia about exactly what the Bible is saying. And this is not just a Christian phenomenon: Jews too, for whom our Old Testament is their scripture, debate for hours over the opinion of this or that famous rabbi.

So how do we work out what it all means? Does the Bible itself give us any guidance in interpretation?

To begin answering that, I'd like to look at the little-known story of Huldah in 2 Chronicles 34. King Josiah, a Good King (as the authors of *1066 and All That* would put it), has decided to make religious reforms. As part of his plan, he has a fund-raising initiative to pay for some building works in the temple. During the handover of the money to the builders, the high priest Hilkiah finds a book lying around in the neglected temple, which he recognizes as 'the book of the law' (v. 15). When the king hears about this, he is distraught, because the people have not been obeying the laws in the book.

What Josiah does next is intriguing. He sends a delegation with the book to 'the prophet Huldah, the wife of Shallum' (v. 22). This female prophet (only the second woman prophet to be found in the Bible) pronounces that this is indeed the book of the law, and that the people will suffer because they have not obeyed it. The king will be spared, however, because he has repented. Then Josiah calls an assembly of the people and reads the whole book to them (it was probably Deuteronomy, so it wouldn't have taken more than a day to read).

You could call Huldah the first Bible interpreter, so I have resolved to take her as a role model in my writing of Bible reading notes (although I am amazed at how few Christians have actually heard of her). What does she teach me?

- That the Bible is not just a book to be studied, but a book to be obeyed.
- In fact, it is in obeying that we begin to understand what we find difficult.
- That the Bible is for everyone, not just a 'scholar class'.
- However, we may need the help of those with particular expertise or insight, as we read this ancient collection of books.
- Finally, that women as well as men are qualified to interpret the Bible.

Of course, Huldah is not my only guide in Bible interpretation. There are other principles that I use. I particularly value the ideas I have learned from my years in the Mennonite church, part of the Anabaptist tradition. From Anabaptist scholars and teachers I have learned that:

- The Bible is not a 'flat' book in which everything can be understood and applied in a similar way. Different types of literature demand different approaches.
- In particular, the Old Testament can no longer be read purely in its own right as a guide to Christian behaviour. It has to be read in the light of the New, because we are not under law, but under grace. To put this more specifically, Jesus is what the early Anabaptists called the 'key of David'—the one whose teachings and life help us unlock the whole of scripture. Jesus is the ultimate Word of God, and any interpretation that does not fit with our understanding of him is probably wrong.
- The best understanding of scripture is gained within the faith community, studying and following together. Understanding the Bible is a corporate, not an individual, process.

Because we cannot know the whole of God's wisdom, there will always be good and bad interpretations. You might say that one of Huldah's predecessors in interpreting a communication from God was the serpent in Eden, who reinterpreted God's one and only command to suit its own purposes!

I get upset when I hear the Bible being abused—used to maintain power over others, used to justify inequality, used in a way that I believe contradicts its main themes of justice, peace, love and community. I get upset, too, when people interpret the Bible in ways that I think are directly contrary to the values of Jesus.

This anger arises because I love the Bible. It's a treasure trove of compelling stories, practical sense, deep wisdom, spiritual insight and passionate prayer. I love writing about the Bible, too. I find it fascinating to read the insights of scholars who have studied its history, its structure and its language. I've been a Christian for over 35 years, and have been writing and editing Bible notes for 25 of them, but no matter how many times I read even the most familiar passage, there always seems to be new meaning and guidance to be gained.

But why do we read the Bible at all? What makes this ancient text more relevant to us than, say, Homer's *Iliad* or the Anglo-Saxon poem *Beowulf*?

Well, a good case could be made for reading it just for its literary merit; after all, it has some of the best stories, and most beautiful imagery, in all of human literature. And it deals with the same major themes of the human condition as other great writings: relationships, war and peace, death, the purpose of life. The late broadcaster John Peel used to read the Bible almost every day, not because he was a Christian (he wasn't) but simply for its literary beauty.

Christians, however, discover a deeper dimension, a sense that this ancient collection of books speaks to us at the core of our spirit, that it stirs and challenges us in a mysterious way. The translator J.B. Phillips started to read the New Testament as a sceptic; yet, as he read, he felt something he could only describe as the ring of truth.

As we allow these time-honoured stories to speak to us, we also discover, if we listen well, that there are all sorts of connections between that long-ago time and ours. Culture may be different, laws may be different, but human beings face much the same choices, dilemmas, problems and opportunities as they did then. We may have discovered how to travel in space, but we are still foreigners in our own internal space—the space where we find God and our true selves.

Ultimately, I believe that we as followers of Jesus need to read the Bible regularly for the same reason that the twelve disciples refused to leave Jesus when others were finding his teaching too hard (John 6:67–68): it has the words of life. If Bible reading aids reveal its life and avoid quenching it, that's probably the best they can do. I hope mine do that for you.

Our Bible reading, however, will be useless unless we learn how to connect what we read with the lives we are living. Jesus himself talked about understanding 'the signs of the times' (Matthew 16:2–3), making the link between the wisdom of old and what is happening around us. I think that is what Huldah was doing, and it is what I aspire to do in writing Bible reading notes.

In the interests of making that link, I have included in this book a selection of the columns that I have written for *Woman Alive* magazine (formerly *Christian Woman*) over more than 20 years; most of them relating directly or indirectly to the themes in the rest of the book. They offer an off-centre view of life as we (or at least I) live it. It's a rollercoaster of a journey, sometimes soaring up, sometimes crashing down, but with the Bible's insights in our hands and hearts, it could be the time of our lives.

THE TIME MACHINE

THE GIFT OF THE BIBLE

Reading the Bible can be rather like entering a time machine. Like Dr Who's (newly revived) Tardis, it takes us to another time and place—a more dim and distant one than any the good Doctor has visited. 'The past is another country,' says classic novelist L.P. Hartley in *The Go-Between*. 'They do things differently there.' They do indeed, which is why we might need a guide as we explore this strange country of the past, and as we ask ourselves what we can learn from it in our own time and place.

One guide that may be useful is what the Bible says about itself—which is what I look at in this first section. The Bible speaks of itself using many images: a lamp, a voice, a path, a sword. It talks of its words being as sweet as honey, but also as a raging fire or a bitter taste. These images seem to express the 'double-edged' nature of the Bible: it reassures and challenges; it rebukes and encourages. If C.S. Lewis' Aslan is 'not a tame lion', this is not a tame book! Sometimes it reminds me of the *Monster Book of Monsters* that Hagrid gives Harry Potter in *The Prisoner of Azkaban*—a book that Harry has to bind with a belt to stop it biting.

I fear that, at times, we have done exactly that with the Bible—tied it up and tamed it so that people actually believe it's about religion rather than about human life and the meaning of life. It's not a collection of holy regulations: it's a book full of comedy, tragedy, and (dare I say) sex and violence. If it were published today for the first time, the church might want to ban it!

In these notes, I have not tried to tell the story of the Bible. Instead I have explored various aspects of how I think it is best interpreted, and how it 'works' in our lives. I found that the Bible itself gives us a lot of guidance on how to read and understand it. The bottom line is: it's all about Jesus. It builds up to him, reveals him, shows us his significance, brings us into relationship with him, and shows us how to live like him. If you read it with him in mind, you can't go too far wrong.

— 1 —

A MASTER KEY

HEBREWS 1:1–3

Long ago God spoke to our ancestors in many and various ways by the prophets, but in these last days he has spoken to us by a Son, whom he appointed heir of all things, through whom he also created the worlds. He is the reflection of God's glory and the exact imprint of God's very being, and he sustains all things by his powerful word.

Hans Denck, a 16th-century Anabaptist, wrote, 'I value Scripture above all things, but not so highly as the Word of God.' What on earth was he getting at?

In everyday talk we may refer to the Bible as 'the word of God', but actually this is inaccurate. Jesus, as the Bible itself tells us, is the living Word, of which the Bible is only a record. 'In the beginning was the Word, and the Word was with God, and the Word was God' (John 1:1).

We need to remember this when we get all het up about our differing interpretations of scripture. Of course it is essential to work out how God wants us to live, but if we do not debate the issues in the peace-making spirit of Christ, we are already disobeying God.

This passage from the beginning of Hebrews is my personal charter for interpreting the Bible—what scholars call a 'hermeneutical key' (hermeneutics is the science of interpretation). I believe that God gradually revealed truths about God and the world to the Jewish people, according to what they were capable of understanding. They wrote down what God revealed, not by a kind of 'automatic writing', but in the language and imagery of their own day.

The greatest revelation of God's nature, however, came when God appeared as a human being, living a human life. So we cannot any longer approach any scripture independently of that life: it is our key to unlock this ancient collection of books. The whole Bible must be read in the light of Jesus, the Word of God. It is his Spirit who will lead us into all truth.

REFLECTION

'Then beginning with Moses and all the prophets, he interpreted to them the things about himself in all the scriptures' (Luke 24:27).

—— 2 ——

MORE THAN USEFUL

2 TIMOTHY 3:14–17

But as for you, continue in what you have learned and firmly believed, knowing from whom you learned it, and how from childhood you have known the sacred writings that are able to instruct you for salvation through faith in Christ Jesus. All scripture is inspired by God and is useful for teaching, for reproof, for correction, and for training in righteousness, so that everyone who belongs to God may be proficient, equipped for every good work.

The Bible makes some mind-blowing claims about Jesus. He is 'the image of the invisible God, the firstborn of all creation… He himself is before all things, and in him all things hold together' (Colossians 1:15, 17). In contrast to this, the claims it makes for itself appear quite humble: it is, like the slave Onesimus (Philemon 11), 'useful'.

Is that all? Is the Bible just a tool in the Christian's toolbox, like a wrench or a spanner? (Admittedly, it must be an infinitely adjustable one, given how we often 'use' it!) Many people prefer to think of it rather as the instruction manual for life—maybe one of those 'home health' books where you can look up any ailment.

Personally I think that even to regard the Bible as a sort of 'handy home book of everything', an encyclopedia of the good life, is to short-change it. Look more closely at what Paul says to Timothy. What does it mean to be 'instructed for salvation'? In the Bible's own view, salvation is much more than a ticket to heaven: it is the total recreation both of ourselves and of the world we live in, so that we and it reflect God's loving values.

And while we are waiting for the new creation, this book is able to 'teach, reprove, correct and train [us] for righteousness'. I don't know a single person who manages to do all those things, yet here Paul is claiming that a book can. That has to be a very special book —not so much an instruction manual as a book of miraculous transformation. No wonder Paul calls it 'the sacred writings' and 'God-breathed' (the literal translation of 'inspired by God'). We'd better read it carefully, then.

PRAYER

'Open my eyes, so that I may behold wondrous things out of your law' (Psalm 119:18).

— 3 —

WORDS OF FIRE

JEREMIAH 20:7–9

O Lord, you have enticed me, and I was enticed; you have overpowered me, and you have prevailed. I have become a laughing-stock all day long; everyone mocks me. For whenever I speak, I must cry out, I must shout, 'Violence and destruction!' For the word of the Lord has become for me a reproach and derision all day long. If I say, 'I will not mention him, or speak any more in his name', then within me there is something like a burning fire shut up in my bones; I am weary with holding it in, and I cannot.

An ancient Chinese poem describes the poet waking up in the night, lighting a lamp and quickly writing down a poem before he forgets it—while his wife looks on, thinking he's mad. I must admit that when I get inspired in the night, I often go back to sleep. Next morning, of course, the poem is completely gone!

The words that Jeremiah feels compelled to speak here are not so easily forgotten. They are a fire in his bones; they burst out of him, against his will. Perhaps this is a better image for how the Bible is inspired than the image of a scribe sitting down and taking God's dictation.

The words of the Bible arise out of passion: a passion for God, the passion of God. This book, or rather this library of books, is a record of things that just *had* to be said. When we read the Bible in church, we often use a solemn, 'flat' voice; some Christian traditions even recommend this, so that the humanity of the reader will not get in the way of the message. But human and divine emotions are what the Bible is all about. When we open it, fire should spring out of its pages and enter our blood. As you prepare to read 'the lesson' in church, feel the fire in it, so that you can convey it to your hearers.

REFLECTION

'I was silent and still; I held my peace to no avail; my distress grew worse, my heart became hot within me. While I mused, the fire burned; then I spoke with my tongue' (Psalm 39:2–3). What might God be asking you to speak out about?

— 4 —

FROM SPEECH TO WRITING

JEREMIAH 36:1–6

In the fourth year of King Jehoiakim son of Josiah of Judah, this word came to Jeremiah from the Lord: Take a scroll and write on it all the words that I have spoken to you against Israel and Judah and all the nations, from the day I spoke to you, from the days of Josiah until today. It may be that when the house of Judah hears of all the disasters that I intend to do to them, all of them may turn from their evil ways, so that I may forgive their iniquity and their sin.

Then Jeremiah called Baruch son of Neriah, and Baruch wrote on a scroll at Jeremiah's dictation all the words of the Lord that he had spoken to him. And Jeremiah ordered Baruch, saying, 'I am prevented from entering the house of the Lord; so you go yourself, and on a fast day in the hearing of the people in the Lord's house you shall read the words of the Lord from the scroll that you have written at my dictation.'

Behind the written Bible that we have now stands a long oral tradition: prophecies, sayings, stories and laws memorized by dedicated people. On this side of the written record stands a long line of translators who made that literature available to us. In the church calendar, on one day each year we commemorate St Jerome, a fourth-century scholar who spent at least four years in the desert, teaching himself Hebrew. Then, with the Greek he already knew, he was able to translate both Old and New Testaments into Latin, the common European language of the time.

If you can do it, reading the Bible in its original languages can be very illuminating. But from the earliest days of the church, the leaders wanted to make the Bible's treasures available to as many different people-groups as possible, in their own words and idioms. The same wish motivates Bible translators today.

As an occasional translator myself (from German), I know how hard it can be to find just the right equivalent word or phrase. Let's be grateful for those, like Jerome, who laboured to give us God's wisdom.

REFLECTION

'Many of the Jews read this inscription, because the place where Jesus was crucified was near the city; and it was written in Hebrew, in Latin, and in Greek' (John 19:20).

---— 5 ---—

NOT EASILY SILENCED

JEREMIAH 36:14–28 (ABRIDGED)

Then all the officials sent Jehudi son of Nethaniah son of Shelemiah son of Cushi to say to Baruch, 'Bring the scroll that you read in the hearing of the people, and come.' ... When they heard all the words, they turned to one another in alarm, and said to Baruch, 'We certainly must report all these words to the king.' ... Now the king was sitting in his winter apartment (it was the ninth month), and there was a fire burning in the brazier before him. As Jehudi read three or four columns, the king would cut them off with a penknife and throw them into the fire in the brazier, until the entire scroll was consumed in the fire that was in the brazier...

Now, after the king had burned the scroll with the words that Baruch wrote at Jeremiah's dictation, the word of the Lord came to Jeremiah: Take another scroll and write on it all the former words that were in the first scroll, which King Jehoiakim of Judah has burned.

Imagine you spent weeks writing a report for work, and then, before you had backed the document up, you accidentally hit the wrong computer key and deleted the lot. Aaargh!

How would Jeremiah feel when Baruch brought him the news of the king's drastic editing methods? Worse than that, I'm sure. But he simply goes to work and dictates all his prophecies to Baruch again—which is why we now have them.

What this story says to me is that there is something enduring about the Bible. These age-old stories, from a culture different from ours in so many ways, somehow still echo across the centuries and shed new light on our daily living for God's kingdom. Even under regimes where possession of a Bible is a criminal offence, God has not been silenced. People have smuggled in Bibles; people have memorized as much of the Bible as they could. It reminds me of Jesus asking the disciples, 'Do you also wish to go away?' and their reply: 'To whom can we go? You have the words of eternal life' (John 6:67–68).

PRAYER

Pray for all for whom the Bible has become a burden, instead of a blessing; pray that they will find new life in its stories.

---- 6 ----

CALL THE FIRST WITNESS

LUKE 1:1–4

> Since many have undertaken to set down an orderly account of the events that have been fulfilled among us, just as they were handed on to us by those who from the beginning were eyewitnesses and servants of the word, I too decided, after investigating everything carefully from the very first, to write an orderly account for you, most excellent Theophilus, so that you may know the truth concerning the things about which you have been instructed.

It was a frosty January morning, and I was driving downhill. Suddenly a car came out from a side road on my left and cut in front of me. I braked with all my might, but still went straight into the other car, doing considerable damage to my new car (and very little to the other driver's).

Shakily, we exchanged addresses and insurance details. I was wondering how I'd get home, since I had no money with me, and the car (let alone myself) was unfit to drive. Suddenly from round the corner emerged another parent from my son's school, where I had just dropped him off. Not only did she offer a lift, but she had seen the whole thing. I had a witness.

Luke's testimony, and that of the other New Testament writers, is not like someone who happened to see a car crash and might get the details wrong. It is more like someone who has studied for three years with a famous teacher, and can now recite all their favourite sayings.

Suppose, if the case had gone to court, that my witness described my car as silver when it was actually gold. That wouldn't affect the truth that the accident wasn't my fault.

23

Similarly, there are some minor contradictions in the Bible, and some stories that have gone through many centuries of retelling and reshaping. God chose to convey truth through fallible human beings. It's also true, however, that these writings have been put together with great care and thought, by God-inspired people who wanted to convey truths about God and life. Some of the facts may be difficult to establish, but truth is not just a matter of facts.

REFLECTION

What kind of truth are you encountering at church?

—— 7 ——

SWEET SOMETHINGS

PSALM 19:7–11

The law of the Lord is perfect, reviving the soul; the decrees of the Lord are sure, making wise the simple; the precepts of the Lord are right, rejoicing the heart; the commandment of the Lord is clear, enlightening the eyes; the fear of the Lord is pure, enduring for ever; the ordinances of the Lord are true and righteous altogether. More to be desired are they than gold, even much fine gold; sweeter also than honey, and drippings of the honeycomb. Moreover by them is your servant warned; in keeping them there is great reward.

Are you one of those people who can always quote the Bible, chapter and verse, for any eventuality of life? I'm not. With me it's more a case of 'It's in Luke somewhere… or it might be in John. Or is it one of the epistles?'

No matter how well you know your way from Adam to Zion, you only really know the Bible when you attempt to live it. Then experience takes over from theory; and at that point, I suspect, we are all equally beginners.

In Juan Carlos Ortiz's book *Disciple* (first published 1975), he describes a novel way of doing Bible study. A discipleship group would read perhaps one verse together and discuss it. Then they would go their separate ways and try to practise it in their lives. The next week they would meet, read the same passage, and discuss how well they had got on with doing it. They would stay in exactly the same place in the Bible until they all felt that they had begun to get to grips with this particular teaching. Only then would they read something new.

This approach doesn't work with all of scripture, of course, since it's not all direct teaching. However, it's a striking way of doing what James tells us: 'Be doers of the word, and not merely hearers... For if any are hearers of the word and not doers, they are like those who look at themselves in a mirror; for they look at themselves and, on going away, immediately forget what they were like' (James 1:22–24).

REFLECTION

God's message is like gold and honey: beautiful and delicious. Do we sometimes make it like granite and lemon: hard and bitter?

A SPECIAL DAY

LUKE 4:16–21

When he came to Nazareth, where he had been brought up, he went to the synagogue on the sabbath day, as was his custom. He stood up to read, and the scroll of the prophet Isaiah was given to him. He unrolled the scroll and found the place where it was written: 'The Spirit of the Lord is upon me, because he has anointed me to bring good news to the poor. He has sent me to proclaim release to the captives and recovery of sight to the blind, to let the oppressed go free, to proclaim the year of the Lord's favour.' And he rolled up the scroll, gave it back to the attendant, and sat down. The eyes of all in the synagogue were fixed on him. Then he began to say to them, 'Today this scripture has been fulfilled in your hearing.'

Just how delighted must Jesus have felt when they gave him the scroll of Isaiah to read from? Each scroll only holds a single Bible book, so the chances of this one being chosen were only 1 in 39. Alternatively, did Jesus perhaps choose to visit this particular synagogue on a day when he knew they would be reading Isaiah?

Either way, what an amazing occasion to be present at: the day when the eternal Word, God's ultimate self-expression, reads and preaches from the written word of the Hebrew scriptures. Even better, to be there when he preaches from Isaiah—the book that contains those marvellous 'servant songs', which later generations would interpret as prophesying the coming of Jesus, among us 'as one who serves' (Luke 22:27).

Yet Jesus chooses not to speak on one of these songs, but on Isaiah's 'social charter' (Isaiah 61). Here at the beginning of his ministry, he declares his priorities: the poor, the imprisoned, the disabled, the oppressed. He also announces a jubilee year, the year when slaves were freed and all land returned to the clans who originally owned it—a year of economic redistribution and justice.

And what is his comment on this passage? 'Today this scripture has been fulfilled in your hearing' (v. 21). In other words, 'This is all about me.' If you hear the Bible being used to justify inequality or oppression, or in any way that marginalizes the agenda of Jesus—be suspicious.

REFLECTION

We are even more privileged than the Nazarenes who heard this sermon: we have the power and opportunity to put it into practice worldwide.

UNPOPULAR INTERPRETATION

LUKE 4:24–27

And [Jesus] said, 'Truly I tell you, no prophet is accepted in the prophet's home town. But the truth is, there were many widows in Israel in the time of Elijah, when the heaven was shut up for three years and six months, and there was a severe famine over all the land; yet Elijah was sent to none of them except to a widow at Zarephath in Sidon. There were also many lepers in Israel in the time of the prophet Elisha, and none of them was cleansed except Naaman the Syrian.'

In an online discussion forum last night, I was discussing whether a church should ever ban an individual from preaching. Some thought all opinions should be heard and discussed; others that preaching should be restricted to those who agreed with all of that church's basis of faith.

If the synagogue at Nazareth had had such a discussion, I think they would have opted for banning Jesus (and indeed, that's just what they did, without any discussion). His use of scripture is provocative to say the least. First of all, he is not preaching from the passage he read, but instead responding to remarks from the congregation. Second, he is more or less saying that God habitually chooses individuals from outside the chosen people to do God's work. No wonder his listeners wanted to kill him!

Jesus' use of the Old Testament (which is frequent) is always bold, creative and thought-provoking—as is the use that the Gospel writers and apostles make of scripture. No tired and worn 'standard' interpretations from them.

The first time I ever preached, it was to a congregation of 450 in a famous charismatic church. Afterwards I heard an elderly lady saying, 'This church is going from bad to worse.' I was consoled by the fact that Jesus' preaching, too, was disliked. I was also heartened by an encounter over coffee with someone who felt excluded by the church, but had felt, for the first time, included by my sermon. My preaching may have been a bit inflammatory, but I think I'd got my priorities right: to focus on the needy, the afraid, those who need comfort most.

PRAYER

Lord, teach those of us who preach to 'disturb the comfortable and comfort the disturbed'.

UNDER YOUR SKIN

JEREMIAH 31:31–33

The days are surely coming, says the Lord, when I will make a new covenant with the house of Israel and the house of Judah. It will not be like the covenant that I made with their ancestors when I took them by the hand to bring them out of the land of Egypt—a covenant that they broke, though I was their husband, says the Lord. But this is the covenant that I will make with the house of Israel after those days, says the Lord: I will put my law within them, and I will write it on their hearts; and I will be their God, and they shall be my people.

Queen Mary Tudor famously said, 'When I am dead and opened, you shall find "Calais" lying in my heart.' So, if you ever need to find Calais…

Bad jokes aside, what might an autopsy find written in our hearts? The metaphorical 'writing' we leave behind us is made up of our deeds and attitudes—and they are made up of what God (or the world) has first written on us.

Jeremiah promises here that one day God's values, the love of God and neighbour, will not be just written in a book but engraved in our spirit. From a visit to Israel I brought back a drawing of Ruth sitting in a cornfield, clutching her gleanings. The whole of Ruth's body in the picture is made up of the book of Ruth, in Hebrew, written in a spiral. I like that as an image of how God's 'law', the priorities and wisdom of God, can seep into us so much that it is in our very bones and bloodstream.

As well as Jerome, the church calendar also honours another Bible translator, William Tyndale, the most influential English translator, whose turn of phrase is still very evident in the King James Bible. He translated into the common tongue of his day, but his 16th-century English is now a foreign language to us. To get the Bible into our system, we need first to hear or read it in words we can understand.

REFLECTION

When the whole of the Bible's wisdom is written into our very veins, we won't need Bibles any more. However, I doubt whether that will be this side of the resurrection!

✛

THE STORY OF A STORY

In my brief career as an editor of Bible reading notes, not just a writer of them, I tried to convey to readers that the Bible is not mainly a collection of laws, commands and instructions, but a collection of time-honoured stories. This column was written shortly after that time, to make the same point.

Once upon a time, there was a story. It lived in a culture—only it preferred to use the term 'people', because it is people who make stories. Though, to be strictly accurate, stories make people, as well as people making stories, and it is not always easy to tell which came first—like chickens and eggs, and I defy you to say who made that one.

Anyway, the story in question made a people, and the people made more stories, and the new stories continued to make the people, until there was quite a collection, both of stories and of people. There were stories about love, and courtship, and marriage, and children, and growing up, and learning, and sowing and harvesting, and feasting and dancing, and building and crafting, and judging and ruling. There were also stories about envy, rape, adultery, murder and revenge; and although these stories were not as nice, they were just as true, because, as one of the earliest stories explained, these are the sort of things that happen when there are people around.

The strangest thing about these stories was that while there were many, they were also one big story. It had a beginning and a middle, and a sort of end—although, according to most of those who told it, the true end was still to come. One could almost say it had lots of little ends that pointed to the great end, and lots of little beginnings too, which all, oddly enough, pointed to the great end as well—or was it the great beginning? You would have to read the story to know what I mean.

Another intriguing thing about this great story was that in between all the little stories, there were things that didn't look much like stories at all. There were songs and poems, laws and instructions, musings and explanations and warnings and sermons. Some of these were quite difficult to understand, but as they went along they were always interrupted by fresh stories—stories about who sang the songs, or about people who broke or kept the laws and what happened to them, or about why and where the sermons were preached and what the people did upon hearing them. This made the whole make sense, and indeed it was clear that all the not-very-storyish bits were there to help the stories, and not (please take note of this) the other way around.

But... something happened to the story. While it was being made (and it took a good long time to make), people mostly handed it on from person to person, direct. One told it to another, and the other told it to a third. And it grew in all sorts of interesting ways as it went along, as all living things must grow if they are to go on living. Then, people discovered that they could draw funny shapes, and that the shapes would stand for sounds, and the sounds would be the sounds of the story, turned into something solid and kept for ever, or almost ever. And this is what they did to the story, and behold, it was a book.

Now the good thing about it being a book was that a lot of people could now have the story at the same time, in different places. And the result was that a lot more people had the story, and the story went on making a people, and it was a much bigger and more exciting people. And another good thing was that when the story was a book, it was easier to make sure that any one people had got the story right, because it no longer changed. And when many people had the book, then they rejoiced because they discovered that, mysteriously, although the book was mainly the story of one particular people, it was also the story of all peoples everywhere—for this was the special power of the special story.

These were the good things about the story becoming a book. There were, however, some very bad things, too. Now that it was a book, those who told it no longer had to tell the whole story to keep it going. They could keep it half shut, or even keep it entirely to themselves, and pass on only the bits that they thought most important, or that they thought would upset things least. The story began to go wrong in various ways.

Many of those who now told it were rulers and masters and husbands and fathers, so they only passed on the bits that were about people like themselves and ignored the bits about subjects and servants and wives and children—except, of course, the bits that encouraged such people to take due notice of rulers and masters and husbands and fathers. Many of the tellers were scholars and lawmakers, who liked rules and instructions and explanations, so they concentrated on those bits and forgot the stories and songs and poems. At best (or worst?) they told the stories in such a way that they turned them into rules and instructions, for they believed that the stories were only there to help the teachings and not (as I told you earlier—remember?) the other way around.

The consequence was that the story became rather boring for many and a source of bondage instead of freedom for some. 'Not that old thing,' said some of those who were called to hear it, and, 'This is not for us—we must write our own story,' said others (for they did not know that it already was their own story, since it had always been told to them as someone else's).

A few brave souls decided that they must bring the story alive again, using all the new and fancy ways they had of preserving sounds and movements and colours and shapes. Sometimes this worked wonderfully, if they had understood what the story was about in the first place (that is, loving and marrying and bearing children and sowing and reaping, and feasting and building and judging and ruling, as well as envy, adultery, murder and forgiving and being forgiven and loving and...). It didn't work so well if they thought the book was about rules and instructions, and that they just had to dress up the rules and instructions in a catchy storyline. Which proves that the story should always come first, and the moral last, if at all.

So there we are. I wonder if you know the story. I wonder if you know it's yours. I hope so, because it's a ripping yarn. Well, more of a mending yarn, actually. Tell it whenever you can.

OLD TIMES

Singer and convert from Judaism, Helen Shapiro, went into a Jewish bookshop soon after her conversion to Christianity and asked for 'an Old Testament'. 'How old?' asked the shopkeeper with typical Jewish wit! To him, of course, it wasn't 'the Old Testament' (since he didn't recognized any new one), but the Tanach, the Hebrew scriptures.

I'm fond of pointing out (perhaps because I'm Jewish) that three-quarters of the Bible was not written by Christians. But what do we, as Christians, do with that three-quarters? Scholars have debated that question ever since the council of Jerusalem (Acts 15), where the very early church had a confab over whether Gentile converts were required to keep the Jewish law as set out in the Jewish scriptures.

A curate at a former church of mine (when I was an accidental Anglican) solved the problem easily: he just rejected the Old Testament outright. He was part of an ancient heritage there: the second-century Christian leader Marcion was excommunicated as a heretic for doing just that. (Christians hadn't started burning or beheading people yet…)

I must confess, I have been tempted at times to follow Marcion's path. I struggle with these books, with their raging, destroying God who seems so different from the Father of Jesus Christ. But there are several reasons why dropping what we call the Old Testament would sell us seriously short as Christians.

First, it would leave us trying to build the 'house' of our Christianity without a foundation. The bigger the building is going to be (and the more inhospitable the ground), the deeper its foundation needs to be. So the church, built with bricks supplied by the New Testament, needs the deep foundation of the Old to ground it.

Second, without the Old Testament we would have great difficulty in understanding Jesus and the Gospels and epistles. Take the Sermon on the Mount, for instance (Matthew 5). Jesus announces, 'You have heard it that it was said to those of ancient times... But I say to you...' How would we understand him correctly if we did not read those sayings of ancient times in their context?

Third, Jesus himself quotes from the Old Testament frequently; and so do the Gospel and epistle writers. Jesus' very first sermon, at the beginning of his ministry, was from Isaiah 61 (see Luke 4:14–27). He clearly thought that God could still speak through the Jewish scriptures; indeed, he probably had no idea that his own words, and accounts of his ministry, would be written down in their turn and become new scriptures. He was a Jew, albeit a radical one, and naturally he preached from the Jewish Bible.

To confirm this, we have Jesus' own statement that 'every scribe who has been trained for the kingdom of heaven is like the master of a household who brings out of his treasure what is new and what is old' (Matthew 13:52). He expected his disciples to be learned both in the Jewish scriptures and in the new ideas he was presenting.

Moreover, we would lose some really good stories if we didn't read the Old Testament!

Finally, if we look closely at the Old Testament, we will find that despite the amount of 'holy war' in it, and despite the dramatic punishments that God inflicts on the disobedient, there is, running through it like a golden thread, 'the Lord, the Lord, a God merciful and gracious, slow to anger, and abounding in steadfast love and faithfulness' (Exodus 34:6). And that is the God we should keep in mind as we read it.

So this section offers some stories from old times—very old times—and attempts to discover how they can still shed light on the times we live in now.

JOSHUA 7—12

'The Old Testament God is totally ruthless,' said an agnostic celebrity in a magazine interview. 'I like that'! If we had only chapters 7—12 of Joshua to tell us about God, we might well agree. This God, who appears to support 'holy war' and 'ethnic cleansing', would be one we might worship but could hardly love.

Indeed, the book has been used in history to justify other genocides in the name of God: the Crusades, the massacre of native Americans by settlers who saw America as their 'promised land' or the domination of South Africa by white colonialists. It also has disturbing resonances with the situation in Israel/Palestine today, and there is plenty of scope for Christians to misuse it in relation to that issue. Is there another way to approach these stories?

It should be said that we do not know whether the massacres happened quite as described. The book probably reached its present form many centuries after the events, although the stories preserved in it are probably more ancient. Some scholars think it was compiled to justify King Josiah's religious reforms and to promote national unity. Nevertheless, this still leaves us with the problem that these chapters show what Israel would have *liked* to do to the Canaanites!

Some people solve it by just extracting the more 'spiritual' passages like 'Be strong and very courageous' (1:7). Some treat it as an allegory of 'spiritual warfare'. Some point out that Canaanite culture, while highly developed (the Canaanites gave us the first alphabet), was bound up with a religion whose worship was 'violently sexual in form' (David Hinson, *History of Israel*, SPCK, 1973). It cannot have been fun being a Canaanite woman!

In grappling with this difficult book, I have discovered many ways in which it can still speak to us today. Moreover, I have gladly recognized that we do not have only this book to tell us about God. In Greek, the name 'Joshua' ('God saves'—the same as 'Hosea') is Iesous, and in Latin, Jesus. I have tried to read Joshua, as I believe we should read all of the Old Testament, with Jesus always in mind.

SELF-DEFEATED

JOSHUA 7:1–5 (ABRIDGED)

But the Israelites broke faith in regard to the devoted things: Achan son of Carmi... took some of the devoted things; and the anger of the Lord burned against the Israelites.

Joshua sent men from Jericho to Ai... and said to them, 'Go up and spy out the land.' ... Then they returned to Joshua and said to him, 'Not all the people need go up...' So about three thousand of the people went up there; and they fled before the men of Ai. The men of Ai killed about thirty-six of them, chasing them from outside the gate as far as Shebarim and killing them on the slope. The hearts of the people melted and turned to water.

Remember the game of 'Simon Says'? Anything the leader tells you to do, you do—unless s/he misses out the vital phrase 'Simon says'. Is God too a game player who waits to catch us out in a misdemeanour, then withdraws his support? Three strikes and you're out? In my worst moments, I sometimes imagine God is like that.

This story might suggest that he is, but the reason for the defeat at Ai goes deeper. Other ancient Near East peoples fighting 'holy war' also destroyed everything as an offering to their gods. The difference with Israel was that they saw God, not Joshua, as the true leader of the conquest. They had this confidence at Jericho, but by now it has turned to complacency: 'God is on our side...'

A guest preacher at my church recently said, 'God's love is both unconditional and deeply conditional.' The picture came to me of a university application. A college may offer an 'unconditional place', not dependent on exam results. But once there, the student must study or be thrown out. I think it was something like that for the

Israelites in Canaan. The land was promised, but they could only 'possess' it—gain and keep it—on condition that they kept God's laws.

Is it the same for Christians? Yes and no. God never stops loving us, but if we do not learn to live the Jesus way, we may stop experiencing that love.

REFLECTION

In what ways does your church help you to live for Christ daily? Take an opportunity this Sunday to thank them.

---- 12 ----

COMPLAINT TO THE MANAGEMENT

JOSHUA 7:7–9 (ABRIDGED)

Joshua said, 'Ah, Lord God! Why have you brought this people across the Jordan at all, to hand us over to the Amorites so as to destroy us? Would that we had been content to settle beyond the Jordan! O Lord, what can I say, now that Israel has turned their backs to their enemies! The Canaanites and all the inhabitants of the land will hear of it, and surround us, and cut off our name from the earth. Then what will you do for your great name?'

I read recently that the most common form of public prayer in the Bible is the prayer of complaint. How about your congregation—is it the most common there? No, mine neither (but we're working on it…)

Joshua's frank conversation with God raises echoes of the Israelites' complaint to Moses: 'If only we had died by the hand of the Lord in the land of Egypt, when we sat by the fleshpots…' (Exodus 16:3). Who did 'die by the hand of the Lord' in Egypt? The Egyptian firstborn. So, in effect, this kind of complaint is saying, 'We wish we were like the other peoples; why do we have to be different?' Joshua, likewise, seems to say, 'Why couldn't we just live where there isn't any opposition?' As Tevye in *Fiddler on the Roof* says, 'Couldn't you just for a moment choose someone else?'

What interests me most, however, is the link that Joshua makes between what happens to Israel and what people think of God. The Canaanites will 'cut off *our* name', and then, Joshua asks God, 'what will you do for *your* great name?' It is as though God's reputation is intimately bound up with the reputation of the people whom God has called.

We know that if we do not do God's will, God will use others: 'God is able from these stones to raise up children to Abraham' (Luke 3:8). Nevertheless, what people think of the church will often be what they think of the church's God. All the more important, then, that we obey his command to 'bear fruits worthy of repentance' (Luke 3:8).

A WAY TO PRAY

Next time things go badly, express yourself frankly to God. You may be surprised at the answer!

—— 13 ——

THE WAGES OF DISOBEDIENCE

JOSHUA 7:10–15 (ABRIDGED)

The Lord said to Joshua, 'Stand up! Why have you fallen upon your face? Israel has sinned; they have transgressed my covenant that I imposed on them. They have taken some of the devoted things... Therefore the Israelites are unable to stand before their enemies; they turn their backs to their enemies, because they have become a thing devoted for destruction themselves... In the morning therefore you shall come forward tribe by tribe... And the one who is taken as having the devoted things shall be burned with fire, together with all that he has, for having transgressed the covenant of the Lord, and for having done an outrageous thing in Israel.'

'If I may speak frankly...' Do you dread it when someone says that? It can be a precursor to taking us down a peg! But sometimes, when we take a deep breath and state our true feelings, it is the beginning of healing in a relationship.

Joshua's frank complaint had an element of 'Why can't we just be like the others?' God gives an equally robust answer: by disobeying his command, the people have indeed become like their enemies—like them in that they're headed for destruction. As dogs become like their owners (or vice versa?), we become like what we value most. Psalm 135:18 says of 'dumb' idols, 'Those who make them and all who trust them shall become like them.'

The Israelites have become like their enemies in another respect too: where the people of Jericho 'melted in fear' before them (Joshua 2:24), now the Israelites likewise 'melt' before the much smaller population of Ai (7:5). The only cure is to fear God instead, for that is 'the beginning of wisdom' (Proverbs 9:10).

For Christians, though, I'm not sure that the word 'fear' is appropriate any more. Instead we love God and our neighbours, for God first loved us (1 John 4:19), and 'there is no fear in love… for fear has to do with punishment' (1 John 4:18). Ancient Israel, in their fear of sinning even accidentally, used the 'scapegoat' to bear the penalty for any unknown sins among the people. There is no more punishment when another has taken the blame.

REFLECTION

We who follow the sin-bearer should never 'scapegoat' anyone else.

---- 14 ----

ONE FOR ALL

JOSHUA 7:19–25 (ABRIDGED)

Then Joshua said to Achan, 'My son, give glory to the Lord God of Israel and make confession to him...' And Achan answered Joshua, 'It is true; I am the one who sinned against the Lord God of Israel... when I saw among the spoil a beautiful mantle from Shinar, and two hundred shekels of silver, and a bar of gold weighing fifty shekels, then I coveted them and took them...'. Then Joshua and all Israel with him took Achan son of Zerah... with his sons and daughters, with his oxen, donkeys, and sheep, and his tent and all that he had; and they brought them up to the Valley of Achor. Joshua said, 'Why did you bring trouble on us? The Lord is bringing trouble on you today.' And all Israel stoned him to death.

The other day I trapped my thumb in a wardrobe door, while standing, at my seven-year-old son's request, on an upturned washing-basket (don't ask!). As I yelled in pain, I tried to reassure John that it wasn't all his fault. But he kept saying, 'Blame me, blame me, then I'll feel better.'

In troubles, we always feel better for finding someone to blame (see Jonah 1). This is how dictators justify purges and genocides. In this story, however, there really is a culprit. Achan's guilt has apparently been discovered by lot, as Jonah's was (Jonah 1:7). Israel's faith is that God will provide; but Achan feels that he needs to provide for himself.

His execution, with his whole family, seems harsh to us. For ancient Israel, however, sin affected a whole family (see Jeremiah 31:29). More than this, one person's self-centredness could threaten the whole community. Notice how our first reading in this section

47

said, 'But *the Israelites* broke faith' (7:1). The story of Ananias and Sapphira in Acts 5 is a New Testament parallel.

The balance between community and individual is always difficult. Perhaps, for any group just establishing itself, community must come first. Have we in the affluent West allowed the balance to swing too far the other way?

PRAYER

'I will... make the Valley of Achor [Trouble] a door of hope' (Hosea 2:15). Use this verse from the book of Joshua's namesake to pray for any area of trouble in the world.

15

THE LORD GIVES...

JOSHUA 8:1, 15–21 (ABRIDGED)

Then the Lord said to Joshua, 'Do not fear or be dismayed; take all the fighting men with you, and go up now to Ai...

Joshua and all Israel made a pretence of being beaten before them, and fled in the direction of the wilderness. So all the people who were in the city were called together to pursue them...

Then the Lord said to Joshua, 'Stretch out the sword that is in your hand towards Ai; for I will give it into your hand.' ... As soon as he stretched out his hand, the troops in ambush rose quickly out of their place and rushed forward.... When Joshua and all Israel saw that the ambush had taken the city and that the smoke of the city was rising, then they turned back and struck down the men of Ai.

William the Conqueror defeated the Saxons in 1066 with exactly Joshua's technique: a fake withdrawal and ambush. In Joshua's case, however, the stratagem was given directly by God.

Joshua's holding up his sword is more than a convenient signal. The sword stays up till the end of the battle, just as Moses' staff was held up while Joshua fought the Amalekites (Exodus 17). The conclusion of that story is Moses' statement, 'The Lord will have war with Amalek from generation to generation' (v. 16). Perhaps we are meant to draw the same conclusion here—that the real conqueror is God. No part of Canaan could be conquered unless God chose to give it. In his book *Yahweh is a Warrior* (Herald Press, 1980), Millard Lind points out how the Israelites deliberately limited their military strength to demonstrate that their true leader in battle was God.

Are Christians today, however, justified in seeing any people as deserving destruction? The people of God now are not a nation, but those who follow the Prince of Peace. We must beware, therefore, of identifying any of today's power politics with God. A better response to these readings from Joshua would be to consider how today we could demonstrate that we too rely on God's power, not on military might.

REFLECTION

Emperor Constantine saw a cross in the sky and heard, 'In this sign you will conquer.' He went on to win in battle. But did he interpret his vision rightly?

16

PROMISES TO KEEP

JOSHUA 8:30–34 (ABRIDGED)

Then Joshua built on Mount Ebal an altar to the Lord, the God of Israel, just as Moses the servant of the Lord had commanded... And there, in the presence of the Israelites, Joshua wrote on the stones a copy of the law of Moses... All Israel, alien as well as citizen, with their elders and officers and their judges, stood on opposite sides of the ark in front of the levitical priests... half of them in front of Mount Gerizim and half of them in front of Mount Ebal, as Moses the servant of the Lord had commanded at the first, that they should bless the people of Israel. And afterwards he read all the words of the law, blessings and curses, according to all that is written in the book of the law.

Now and then (when I remember), I reread the Anglican wedding service to see what I promised. I also reread insurance policies or guarantees occasionally, to see what others have promised me! The two activities are very different. One deals with legal, contractual obligations that I could call on in court. The other is about a personal, voluntary covenant between two parties to do what is best for each other in everything.

The covenant between God and Israel, symbolized here by the ark, is of the 'marriage vows' kind. People have recognized for millennia that a public commitment helps people to survive in a relationship. Similarly, commitment to God's way was to help Joshua's people to live in the promised land.

At the same time, there are differences too. The covenant with Yahweh is not a covenant of equals, so it rightly involves worship, an act expressing reverence and obedience. From the beginning, Israel's leadership was concerned to link living in the land with faithfulness to God's commandments.

In marriage, even when one partner breaks the vows, the other may still want to express faithfulness. So God's faithfulness was able to survive repeated betrayals by God's people. There's hope for us all, then.

REFLECTION

Jesus said to her, 'Woman, believe me, the hour is coming when you will worship the Father neither on this mountain nor in Jerusalem... But the hour is coming, and is now here, when the true worshippers will worship the Father in spirit and truth' (John 4:21, 23).

17

FALSE FRIENDS

JOSHUA 9:3–6, 14–15 (ABRIDGED)

But when the inhabitants of Gibeon heard what Joshua had done to Jericho and to Ai, they… went and prepared provisions, and took worn-out sacks for their donkeys, and wineskins, worn-out and torn and mended, with worn-out, patched sandals on their feet, and worn-out clothes; and all their provisions were dry and mouldy. They went to Joshua in the camp at Gilgal, and said to him and to the Israelites, 'We have come from a far country; so now make a treaty with us.' … So the leaders partook of their provisions, and did not ask direction from the Lord. And Joshua made peace with them, guaranteeing their lives by a treaty; and the leaders of the congregation swore an oath to them.

Like Rahab in the story of Jericho, the people of Gibeon decide that discretion is the better part of valour. There is a contrast, however, with her apparently genuine belief that God was in the Israelites' invasion: 'I know that the Lord has given you the land' (Joshua 2:9). The Gibeonites' 'Your servants have come from a very far country, because of the name of the Lord your God' rings less true. If the first part of the statement is a lie, how can we believe the second?

The Israelites, meanwhile, leave God entirely out of their calculations. Perhaps they are rather tired of fighting and feel that an alliance dropped into their laps is not to be sneezed at, wherever it comes from. It's a fine line between 'Whoever is not against us is for us' (Mark 9:40) and 'Whoever is not with me is against me' (Matthew 12:30).

This story alerts us to two extremes. One is to 'take the name of the Lord in vain', which I think refers less to swearing than to tacking the name of God on to your activities in order to fend off all criticism. This is what the Gibeonites did. The other is to act without any real reference to God, whether you justify your actions by 'common sense', 'that's the way the world is', or whatever. This is what Israel did. Which extreme is your usual temptation?

PRAYER

'Unless the Lord builds the house, those who build it labour in vain' (Psalm 127:1). Bring any plans you have to God in your prayers.

—— 18 ——

COUNT ME IN

JOSHUA 9:22–27 (ABRIDGED)

Joshua summoned them, and said to them, 'Why did you deceive us, saying, "We are very far from you", while in fact you are living among us?' ... They answered Joshua, 'Because it was told to your servants for a certainty that the Lord your God had commanded his servant Moses to give you all the land, and to destroy all the inhabitants of the land before you; so we were in great fear for our lives because of you, and did this thing. And now we are in your hand: do as it seems good and right in your sight to do to us.' This is what he did for them: he saved them from the Israelites; and they did not kill them. But on that day Joshua made them hewers of wood and drawers of water for the congregation and for the altar of the Lord, to continue to this day, in the place that he should choose.

'Are they Christian?' asked an old friend when she heard that my husband and I had joined the Mennonite church. Every human group likes to have boundaries, to know who is in and who is out, to check new members for 'soundness'.

The Gibeonites were followers of Canaanite religion, with which the Israelites were to have no compromise. Yet because of their 'cunning plan', based on fear of God, not love, they find themselves permanently under contract to serve the practical needs of Israelite worship. Are they 'in' or 'out'? Perhaps God does not always draw the boundaries in the same places as we do. In Joshua we see a Jericho prostitute saved (chapter 6), but a faithless Israelite destroyed (chapter 7). Inclusion or exclusion seems to have more to do with whether you go God's way than whether you name God's name.

Is it different in the New Testament, where we are 'justified by faith' (Romans 3:28)? Paul himself says no. Believers are included in the faith community by God's grace, but also for a purpose: 'For we are what he has made us, created in Christ Jesus for good works, which God prepared beforehand to be our way of life' (Ephesians 2:10). We believe, then we follow—but for some, it may well be the other way round.

PRAYER

Inclusive God, may our churches be places where the unsure, the seeking, the fearful are welcomed.

— 19 —

FRIENDS IN HIGH PLACES?

JOSHUA 10:1–6 (ABRIDGED)

When King Adoni-zedek of Jerusalem heard how Joshua had taken Ai, and had utterly destroyed it… and how the inhabitants of Gibeon had made peace with Israel and were among them, he became greatly frightened, because Gibeon was a large city… and all its men were warriors. So King Adoni-zedek of Jerusalem sent a message to King Hoham of Hebron, to King Piram of Jarmuth, to King Japhia of Lachish, and to King Debir of Eglon, saying, 'Come up and help me, and let us attack Gibeon; for it has made peace with Joshua and with the Israelites.' … And the Gibeonites sent to Joshua at the camp in Gilgal, saying, 'Do not abandon your servants; come up to us quickly, and save us, and help us.'

A couple of years ago, I prayed for more friends. After my cancer diagnosis I found out how many friends I already had!

They say it's not what you know that matters; it's who you know. Slavery in ancient Israel conferred obligations on the owner, too, so the Gibeonites here are able to turn to Israel for help.

Israel itself, however, must not depend on alliances with powerful neighbours: 'Alas for those who go down to Egypt for help… who trust in chariots because they are many and in horsemen because they are very strong, but do not look to the Holy One of Israel or consult the Lord!' (Isaiah 31:1). On the contrary, in the coming kingdom, all other peoples will look to God's people for guidance: 'Thus says the Lord of hosts: In those days ten men from nations of every language shall take hold of a Jew, grasping his garment and saying, "Let us go with you, for we have heard that God is with you"' (Zechariah 8:23).

Are Christians renowned for our better way of life? A week ago as I write, twelve thousand people, many Christian, met outside Parliament to lobby for justice in world trade. MPs received their information with gratitude. Meanwhile, Mennonite and Quaker churches are becoming experts in conflict mediation. If we are professional peacemakers, the world may beat a path to our door.

REFLECTION

Is your church friends with your local MP or a campaigning group? If not, why not? Pray today for Christians with political influence.

—— 20 ——

SOMETHING NEW UNDER THE SUN

JOSHUA 10:8–13 (ABRIDGED)

The Lord said to Joshua, 'Do not fear them, for I have handed them over to you; not one of them shall stand before you.' So Joshua came upon them suddenly, having marched up all night from Gilgal. And the Lord threw them into a panic before Israel, who inflicted a great slaughter on them... As they fled before Israel... the Lord threw down huge stones from heaven on them as far as Azekah, and they died; there were more who died because of the hailstones than the Israelites killed with the sword.

On the day when the Lord gave the Amorites over to the Israelites, Joshua spoke to the Lord; and he said in the sight of Israel, 'Sun, stand still at Gibeon, and Moon, in the valley of Aijalon.' And the sun stood still, and the moon stopped, until the nation took vengeance on their enemies.

Have you ever prayed for something really crazy? I don't mean, 'Lord, move this paperclip by my faith', but something you deeply wanted but which seemed impossible.

Joshua's 'crazy' prayer is for something to help him in his defeat of the Amorites. From the positions of sun and moon described, he may have been asking for an extension of night, rather than day; which would also explain the Amorites' panic.

Is this a historical event or a poetic image of God's involvement in the battle? For God, nothing is impossible (Matthew 19:26) and Jesus promised that even a mustard seed-sized faith would move mountains (Matthew 17:20). Whether history or myth, however, the point is the same: the battle against these five southern warlords was God's, not Israel's. Notice how the writer stresses that more died from the natural (or supernatural?) disaster than by the swords of Israel.

I hope we do not wish our prayers to be answered by the slaughter of our enemies, for we are commanded to love them (Matthew 5:44). We all have 'impossibilities' in our lives, however. Our battle is not against human beings, but 'spiritual forces of evil in the heavenly places' (Ephesians 6:12). This story's picture of 'something happening in the heavens' can encourage us to use spiritual, not physical, weapons.

PRAYER

Bring your biggest 'impossibility' to God today.

THOSE WHO LIVE BY THE SWORD

JOSHUA 10:16–18, 22–26 (ABRIDGED)

Meanwhile… it was told Joshua, 'The five kings have been found, hidden in the cave at Makkedah.' Joshua said, 'Roll large stones against the mouth of the cave, and set men by it to guard them…

Then Joshua said, 'Open the mouth of the cave, and bring those five kings out to me from the cave.' … Joshua summoned all the Israelites, and said to the chiefs of the warriors who had gone with him, 'Come near, put your feet on the necks of these kings.' … And Joshua said to them, 'Do not be afraid or dismayed; be strong and courageous; for thus the Lord will do to all the enemies against whom you fight.' Afterwards Joshua struck them down and put them to death, and he hung them on five trees.

In the film *No Man's Land*, about the Bosnian war, two opposing soldiers are trapped in an abandoned trench, while a third, who had been thought dead, is lying on a 'bouncing mine' which will kill all three if he moves. The film ends with a retreating shot of the one man left alone, lying there, after the two others have shot each other. He seemed to me to be a metaphor of the land, torn apart by war.

The 'kings' in the Bible passage here were probably no more than local warlords—a term that, ten years ago, might have had an antiquated ring, but now sounds terrifyingly topical. We can imagine how terrified the five warlords would be, trapped in the 'black hole' of the cave. They in turn had terrified others, before Joshua terrified them… and so the cycle goes on.

Perhaps the symbolic action of feet on necks stands for more than just the defeat of five small warlords by a stronger one, however. Perhaps we can take it as a sign of what God plans to do with the whole system of terror and military subjugation: to trample it under God's feet. Even under the old covenant there is a glimpse of the final peace: 'He makes wars cease to the end of the earth; he breaks the bow, and shatters the spear; he burns the shields with fire' (Psalm 46:9).

REFLECTION

'Stop fighting, and know that I am God' (song by Andrew Kreider, based on Psalm 46:10).

---— 22 ---—

SPIRITUAL WEAPONS

JOSHUA 11:1–6 (ABRIDGED)

When King Jabin of Hazor heard of this, he sent to King Jobab of Madon, to the king of Shimron, to the king of Achshaph, and to the kings who were in the northern hill country, and in the Arabah south of Chinneroth, and in the lowland, and in Naphoth-dor on the west, to the Canaanites in the east and the west, the Amorites, the Hittites, the Perizzites, and the Jebusites in the hill country, and the Hivites under Hermon in the land of Mizpah. They came out, with all their troops, a great army, in number like the sand on the seashore, with very many horses and chariots...

And the Lord said to Joshua, 'Do not be afraid of them, for tomorrow at this time I will hand over all of them, slain, to Israel; you shall hamstring their horses, and burn their chariots with fire'.

If you've been on pilgrimage to Israel, you've probably seen the excavations at Hazor. It was a large fortified city with room to keep many horses and chariots as well as perhaps 40,000 people within its walls—a political and military base combined. Under its king, another alliance is formed against the Israelites, this time of northern 'kings'.

What would an ordinary military commander do on capturing a city full of the latest weaponry and military transport (for 'horses and chariots' read 'tanks and warheads')? Most probably, he'd readily accept this free gift to the defence budget. Israel under God's command, however, is ordered to destroy everything—chariots and the horses that power them. Horses were military animals, but the preferred mount for the Prince of Peace is a donkey (Matthew 21:5).

As scholars have pointed out, the only one with a chariot in ancient Israel is God: 'You make the clouds your chariot, you ride on the wings of the wind' (Psalm 104:3). Once again we are to learn that 'Joshua took all these kings and their land at one time, *because the Lord God of Israel fought for Israel*' (Joshua 10:42). Not 'fought with', but 'fought *for*': the victories are seen as entirely God's doing.

PRAYER

Lord, help us to see what you are doing in today's conflicts and issues; and to join in, with your spiritual weapons.

23

LAND RIGHTS

JOSHUA 11:18–23

Joshua made war a long time with all those kings... For it was the Lord's doing to harden their hearts so that they would come against Israel in battle, in order that they might be utterly destroyed, and might receive no mercy, but be exterminated, just as the Lord had commanded Moses.

At that time Joshua came and wiped out the Anakim from the hill country, from Hebron, from Debir, from Anab, and from all the hill country of Judah, and from all the hill country of Israel; Joshua utterly destroyed them with their towns... So Joshua took the whole land, according to all that the Lord had spoken to Moses; and Joshua gave it for an inheritance to Israel according to their tribal allotments. And the land had rest from war.

If the Anakim sound like something from *Star Wars*, it may not be a coincidence! Writers like to borrow exotic-sounding names with mythical associations. The Anakim were the people seen by the spies whom Moses sent into the land, who returned saying, 'All the people that we saw in it are of great size... and to ourselves we seemed like grasshoppers' (Numbers 13:32–33). Only Caleb and Joshua retained their courage: 'If the Lord is pleased with us, he will bring us into this land and give it to us' (14:8).

It is not easy for city dwellers like myself to enter into a full understanding of what land meant for the people of Israel. Buying our food from supermarkets, we forget our dependence on the land and what it can produce. Yet without access to land to grow crops and raise animals, we would all starve.

For the refugee Israelites, God's promised gift of 'a land that flows with milk and honey' (Numbers 14:8) meant the difference between life and death. The same is true for most refugees today.

What problems feel like (or perhaps really are) 'life and death' issues to you? We no longer need to say, 'If the Lord is pleased with us', for if we are in Christ, God says to all of us, 'This is my beloved child, with whom I am well pleased' (Matthew 3:17, adapted).

PRAYER

Pray for those driven from their land, that our own and other safe lands may be welcoming to them, and that all lands may have rest from war.

24

WAYS OF REJOICING

JOSHUA 12:7–24 (ABRIDGED)

The following are the kings of the land whom Joshua and the Israelites defeated on the west side of the Jordan, from Baal-gad in the valley of Lebanon to Mount Halak, that rises towards Seir (and Joshua gave their land to the tribes of Israel as a possession according to their allotments...): the king of Jericho, one; the king of Ai, which is next to Bethel, one; the king of Jerusalem, one; the king of Hebron, one; the king of Jarmuth, one; the king of Lachish, one... the king of Dor in Naphath-dor, one; the king of Goiim in Galilee, one; the king of Tirzah, one—thirty-one kings in all.

As I write, we've just had the World Cup. Everywhere, I saw England flags, drove past pubs full of people spilling out on to the pavement and heard roars of joy or groans of defeat rising.

Joshua's list of kings reads rather like the football results. But it's more serious than that, with its repeated 'one' like a bell tolling the death knell of Canaanite society. Find the chapter and read the whole list aloud to get the full chilling effect.

It's understandable to catalogue and announce one's victories. Notice, however, how God seems to be left out of this account... Then contrast how Paul chronicles his 'victories' in 2 Corinthians 11:24–27: five lots of 39 lashes, three beatings, a stoning, shipwreck, in danger from Gentiles, from false brothers and sisters, hungry, thirsty, cold... rather a different kind of 'boasting'!

Now see Jesus just before his death: 'Jesus answered them, "The hour has come for the Son of Man to be glorified"' (John 12:23). Glorified? By experiencing execution on criminal charges? Most of us would rather have the '31 kings defeated' kind of glory than the suffering and death kind. Some churches encourage a 'success' mentality. In the kingdom of God, however, 'victory' has changed its meaning. 'The Son of God was revealed for this purpose', not to destroy peoples, however corrupt, but 'to destroy the works of the devil' (1 John 3:8).

REFLECTION

'My brothers and sisters, whenever you face trials of any kind, consider it nothing but joy' (James 1:2). Meditate on this and pray to learn how to do it.

✢

WHY I AM A MENNONITE

The stories of the Old Testament, especially stories like those in Joshua, present particular problems for Christian pacifists like myself. Actually, being a Christian presents a particular problem for pacifists like myself. The moment I mention my convictions, other Christians seem to want to argue me out of them. It's really not worth trying, since I've held these convictions my whole life—over 50 years now.

I wonder how people would react if I said, 'I support war.' Anyway, the column below is an attempt to explain a little of why I believe that to follow Jesus means to walk the way of peace, nationally as well as individually.

'I'm glad that Palestinian was killed,' said my then six-year-old son, John, on hearing the news of the latest suicide bomber in Israel. 'Now he won't be able to blow up any more people.'

Temporarily dumbstruck, I was stumped for a good answer. I could see his logic. It was only later that I began to marshall my counter-arguments, and by then the moment had passed.

So this is what I would have said, had I thought quicker—along with some more that I wouldn't attempt to say to a six-year-old, but want to say to you.

Yes, that Palestinian did a bad thing. He also did a brave thing, since he knew that he himself would die horribly as a result of his act. His bravery—or desperation—does not make the bad thing any better. Two teenagers died. Because of the way he killed them, he will not kill any more; but, inspired by him, other Palestinians may well do the same thing.

What made him so passionate and despairing about his cause that he would not only kill but also die for it? Presumably, it was partly the (less courageous) acts of violence committed on his own people by his enemies. I sponsor a little girl in a Palestinian village and recently got news of her Christian school. The caretaker's grandchild, a little boy aged four, was standing on his grandfather's balcony when he was hit by an Israeli sniper. He lost an eye—while the snipers were safe behind their parapets.

Yes, Israeli babies have been killed, too, and some might say of the Palestinians, in that well-worn playground phrase, 'They started it.' That, of course, ignores the years of second-class citizenship, poverty, refugee camps and massacres.

But I don't want to get into Israel–Palestine politics. It's a hornet's nest from which I would certainly emerge severely stung. The point I want to make is that the man of whose death John was so glad undoubtedly had a mother and father, sisters and brothers and friends, maybe a wife and children, who will not be glad at all. However much they may think of him with pride as a 'martyr of Islam', they will also wail with grief in that expressive Middle Eastern way, and miss him for the rest of their lives.

Is this war (for war it is, even if you call it a 'crisis' or 'conflict') a just war? Is any war just? Christians have traditionally put many wars, especially the ones they've been involved in, in that category. World War II is the prime example, since just about everyone with a working brain agrees that Hitler was a 'bad thing'.

The trouble is, the 'just war' theory was worked out in the days of bows and arrows, and possibly the odd siege-engine throwing stones. Can it really work with 'smart' bombs (usually not so smart), nuclear devices many times the strength of the Hiroshima one, and our army's latest acquisition, a blinding machine that permanently destroys enemy soldiers' sight with one flash? (Yes, it really is our army that has bought it.)

A just war has to have a just cause. Plenty can pass that test: the prevention of genocide, elimination of a tyrant, defence of national borders. It also has to be unavoidable. By the popular view, World War II passed that one, too. As the child of World War II refugees, I'm not so sure. Maybe much more could have been done—like a less vindictive treaty after the pointless First World War, for instance.

Lastly, a just war should be fought with just means, which do damage only to voluntary combatants and do not cause undue collateral harm to civilians and 'innocent' women and children. No war fought with modern weaponry can pass that test. A century ago, 90 per cent of injury and death in war was inflicted on soldiers. Now, 90 per cent is inflicted on civilians.

But it is not these arguments that convince me in the end that no one who follows Jesus should be engaging in, or supporting, war. In the end, it is purely because I follow the Prince of Peace, who commanded me to love my enemies. I fail to see any way I can love my enemy by killing him or paying others to do so. Hence I support the 'peace tax' campaign.

So, among many other reasons, I am a Mennonite because it is one of the few world churches (in Britain, only ourselves and the Quakers) that is officially and unashamedly pacifist. We support not only non-violence but also active and creative peace-making.

In the end, it comes down to this: if I ask myself the popular question, 'What would Jesus do?' I find I cannot, by any stretch, imagine him with a nuclear warhead or a Kalashnikov. Can you?

OLD TESTAMENT WOMEN

Who are your Old Testament heroes? Try listing five. Were any of them women? If they were, congratulations. If not, you are probably in good company. From Sunday school to seminary, the 'story of the Bible' highlights male hero after male hero. If we're lucky, we get a nod to Ruth as a romantic sideline. If we're unlucky, we get Eve as an example of how unreliable women are!

Yet where would Abraham have been without Sarah? Or Jacob without his wives and concubines? Where would Barak be without Deborah? How would Josiah have coped with the finding of the book of the law without Huldah? (Read about her in 2 Chronicles 34.)

The notes that follow were inspired by reading a *New Daylight* series by Adrian Plass on Old Testament characters. They were entertaining and challenging notes, as always, but every single character was a man. Where were the role models for women? Or, indeed, the awful warnings for women? (I'm rather attached to Jezebel, myself— splendid woman, if only she'd been on God's side.)

Never one to resist a challenge, I set out to write a series on the dynamic, brave and sometimes just devious women of the Old Testament. As I selected characters, I realized that far more than one series of twelve women would be needed. There were dozens! So this series only goes as far as Judges. Maybe there'll be another one in the future.

Unfortunately, owing to general confusion in the paperwork after the sad death of *New Daylight* editor Shelagh Brown, these notes were never published. So I am offering them to you here instead, for the edification of (and occasional dreadful warning to) both women and men.

25

EVE

GENESIS 3:1–6 (ABRIDGED)

Now the serpent was more crafty than any other wild animal that the Lord God had made. He said to the woman, 'Did God say, "You shall not eat from any tree in the garden?" The woman said to the serpent, 'We may eat of the fruit of the trees in the garden; but God said, "You shall not eat of the fruit of the tree that is in the middle of the garden, nor shall you touch it, or you shall die."' But the serpent said to the woman, 'You will not die; for God knows that when you eat of it your eyes will be opened, and you will be like God, knowing good and evil.' So... she took of its fruit and ate; and she also gave some to her husband, who was with her, and he ate.

The Bible is packed with fascinating women, often only glimpsed but very well worth meeting. Hence this small series, which begins with the 'mother of us all'.

Talking snakes and forbidden fruit? Can we take it seriously? Many scholars think we are dealing with myth here: stories about the unknown past that shed light on our present condition. And this one sheds light at all sorts of levels. Not very fairly, Eve has been blamed throughout Judeo-Christian history for the ills of humankind: she is the weaker sex, easily deceived, a temptress and a danger to men's souls.

Yet look at what the tempter actually says: 'You will be like God.' Hang about—isn't Eve *already* like God? Aren't we told in Genesis 1:26 that male and female were made in God's image? If the serpent stands for the devil, then throughout scripture he is known as 'the accuser'; here he accuses Eve of some inadequacy in her nature that doesn't actually exist!

I wrote a poem about this passage, called 'Deception', which contained the lines 'Poor Eve; why won't she realize *right now* she's able, strong and wise / with nothing but the choice of good to gain?' When we think less of ourselves than God does, temptation has an easy way in.

REFLECTION

Are women still told they are less like God than men are? Pray for women who feel inferior, and for those who seek power wrongly in pagan 'goddess' religions.

26

SARAI

GENESIS 12:10–17 (ABRIDGED)

Now there was a famine in the land. So Abram went down to Egypt to reside there as an alien... When he was about to enter Egypt, he said to his wife Sarai, 'I know well that you are a woman beautiful in appearance; and when the Egyptians see you, they will say, "This is his wife"; then they will kill me, but they will let you live. Say you are my sister, so that it may go well with me because of you, and that my life may be spared on your account.' When Abram entered Egypt the Egyptians saw that the woman was very beautiful... And the woman was taken into Pharaoh's house. And for her sake he dealt well with Abram... But the Lord afflicted Pharaoh and his house with great plagues because of Sarai, Abram's wife.

This morning I was reading a review of Naomi Wolf's book *The Beauty Myth* (Vintage, 1991). She is one of many to complain that women are valued, employed and sometimes dismissed purely on the grounds of personal appearance. The term 'sex object' says it all: have you ever heard a man called an object?

It is only after the Fall, in Genesis 3, that Adam names the woman Eve as he has earlier named the animals. Naming is an act of power, almost of ownership; woman has descended from a partner to a possession. So to Abram, Sarai is a necessity to be taken along on the journey but disposed of as soon as she becomes an inconvenience. Only Abram and Pharaoh speak in this story. Sarai is dumb, ordered about like a slave, and we get no hint of her feelings at being shuffled off into Pharaoh's harem.

That was then, we may say; but it was only 130 years ago that the law was changed to allow married women in Britain to keep their own property, while today in some countries young brides are burned to death by their in-laws because they have not brought enough dowry. Meanwhile, many women feel unable to leave violent relationships because they cannot imagine managing alone. Is slavery really dead?

Sarai's silence speaks for every woman who is dealt with as a commodity, from the supermodel to the teenage prostitute enslaved to her pimp and her drugs.

REFLECTION

The name Sarai means 'princess'. The irony is that when we see women as princesses instead of just normal human beings, we are halfway to making them slaves.

27

HAGAR

GENESIS 16:1–13 (ABRIDGED)

Now Sarai, Abram's wife, bore him no children. She had a Egyptian slave-girl whose name was Hagar, and Sarai said to Abram, '… Go in to my slave-girl; it may be that I shall obtain children by her.' … He went in to Hagar, and she conceived; and when she saw that she had conceived, she looked with contempt on her mistress. Then Sarai said to Abram, 'May the wrong done to me be on you!' … But Abram said to Sarai, 'Your slave-girl is in your power; do to her as you please.' Then Sarai dealt harshly with her, and she ran away from her.

The angel of the Lord found her by a spring of water in the wilderness… And he said, 'Hagar, slave girl of Sarai, where have you come from and where are you going?' She said, 'I am running away from my mistress Sarai.' The angel of the Lord said to her, 'Return to your mistress, and submit to her… I will so greatly multiply your offspring that they cannot be counted for multitude.' … So she named the Lord who spoke to her, 'You are El-roi'; for she said, 'Have I really seen God and remained alive after seeing him?'

Sarai's own experience of being handed around does not make her treat her slave any better! But there is blame on both sides: the powerless, given power, becomes the oppressor, while the fertile despises the infertile. Again, we need not look far for contemporary parallels.

It is not to the most virtuous but to the lowest in the pecking order, the exile Hagar, that God chooses to speak. And Hagar responds. She is the first person in the Bible to give a name to God: 'the God of seeing' or 'the God who sees'. Her return to her oppressor is freely undertaken. She has become a person who can make choices other than resignation or angry defiance.

The conflict between the children of Hagar's son, Ishmael, and those of Sarai's son, Isaac, still plays itself out today in the Middle East. Yet both are the fruit of God's promises—something to remember when either party in a conflict thinks God is on their side.

PRAYER

'We are children, not of the slave but of the free woman' (Galatians 4:31). Ponder what true freedom means, and pray for oppressors and the oppressed, that they may find it.

---— 28 ——

SARAH

GENESIS 18:1–2, 9–12 (ABRIDGED)

The Lord appeared to Abraham by the oaks of Mamre, as he sat at the entrance of his tent in the heat of the day. He looked up and saw three men standing near him...

They said to him, 'Where is your wife Sarah?' And he said, 'There, in the tent.' Then one said, 'I will surely return to you in due season, and your wife Sarah shall have a son.' And Sarah was listening at the tent entrance behind him. Now Abraham and Sarah were old, advanced in age; it had ceased to be with Sarah after the manner of women. So Sarah laughed to herself, saying, 'After I have grown old, and my husband is old, shall I have pleasure?'

A friend of mine living in an inner-city area visited her doctor for some minor problem. 'Twenty-six?' he exclaimed, checking her notes. 'You should have had a couple of children by now!' I wonder what he would have said to Sarah? Her story cocks the ultimate snook at the cult of youth, and encourages all of us 'elderly primigravidae' (I had my first and only baby at 41). We need not take the ages of Abraham (100) and Sarah (90) literally to see this story as a miracle.

In a world where childbearing was seen as the whole purpose of women, a childless woman past menopause was what we'd now call 'a waste of space'. No wonder Sarah laughs bitterly. Custom forbids her to meet her husband's guests directly; her job is to prepare the food that he serves. She cannot even receive God's promise directly.

But notice the name changes that God has now given to both husband and wife. Before God can heal us or make us fruitful, he may have to transform our image of ourselves. Change in our character and behaviour can take a little longer; Sarah, when she becomes a mother herself, no longer tolerates the presence of Hagar's son, whose birth had been brought about by her own decisions (see Genesis 21). Like their male counterparts, Old Testament women are complex, neither all good nor all bad.

REFLECTION

'Now Sarah said, "God has brought laughter for me; everyone who hears will laugh with me"' (21:6). Sarah turns from cynical laughter to joyful laughter. What changes in your own life have brought healthy, God-given laughter? Give thanks for them.

REBEKAH

GENESIS 27:5–10

Now Rebekah was listening when Isaac spoke to his son Esau. So when Esau went to the field to hunt for game and bring it, Rebekah said to her son Jacob, 'I heard your father say to your brother Esau, "Bring me game, and prepare for me savoury food to eat, that I may bless you before the Lord before I die." Now therefore, my son, obey my word as I command you. Go to the flock, and get me two choice kids, so that I may prepare from them savoury food for your father, such as he likes; and you shall take it to your father to eat, so that he may bless you before he dies.'

Rebekah's story, like the stories of so many women, begins in romance: 'Isaac brought her into his mother Sarah's tent... and she became his wife; and he loved her. So Isaac was comforted after his mother's death' (Genesis 24:67).

But the trouble, as so often, comes with the birth of the children for whom Isaac has fervently prayed. Conflict between the twins starts in the womb and is reflected in their parents—or is it the other way around? 'Isaac loved Esau... but Rebekah loved Jacob' (25:28). And so to today's story of deception and manipulation.

How have we come from the shy, submissive young girl who, when asked 'Will you go with this man?', simply answered, 'I will', to this scheming, dominating mother? Perhaps there are clues right at the beginning. Isaac's love for Rebekah is tangled up with bereavement at his mother's death; and later, in exile, he repeats his father Abraham's trick of passing her off as his sister (Genesis 26:7). Psychologists observe that family patterns repeat themselves from generation to generation. As Sarah schemed to gain a son by Hagar, so Rebekah schemes to get the paternal blessing for her favourite.

Yet still, through this soap-opera family, God pursues his own plans. Jacob, as much a schemer as his mother, is nevertheless not only Rebekah's choice, but also God's choice to live out his promises. Even our weaknesses can be used in God's redemptive work.

PRAYER

'You're talking just like my/your mother!' Sound familiar? Bring before God any conflict, or repeated patterns, in your own family. Ask that his grace might be shown in the midst of the accusations and plotting.

---- 30 ----

RACHEL AND LEAH

GENESIS 29:31; 30:1–10, 22 (ABRIDGED)

When the Lord saw that Leah was unloved, he opened her womb; but Rachel was barren...

When Rachel saw that she bore Jacob no children, she envied her sister; and she said to Jacob, 'Give me children, or I shall die! ... So she gave him her maid Bilhah as a wife... And Bilhah conceived and bore Jacob a son... When Leah saw that she had ceased bearing children, she took her maid Zilpah and gave her to Jacob as a wife. Then Leah's maid Zilpah bore Jacob a son...

Then God remembered Rachel, and God heeded her and opened her womb.

The soap opera continues! Rachel and Leah's antagonism begins when their father Laban gives Leah to Jacob instead of the promised Rachel, and it issues in a decades-long childbearing contest. The comments of the two wives tell the whole tragic story:

Leah, after her firstborn: 'Surely now my husband will love me'; after her second: 'Because the Lord has heard that I am hated, he has given me this son'; and even after her sixth, she still hopes pathetically: 'God has endowed me with a good dowry; now my husband will honour me' (Genesis 29:32, 33; 30:20).

Rachel, after her maid has borne two sons: 'With mighty wrestlings I have wrestled with my sister, and have prevailed' (what an ironic echo of Jacob's wrestling with God!). And again, when she herself has given birth, 'God has taken away my reproach... May the Lord add to me another son!' But the next child causes her death; and she names him Ben-oni, 'son of my sorrow' (30:8, 23–24; 35:18).

The unwanted woman and the infertile wife—their painful story illustrates just how much women may invest in marriage and childbirth. Unwillingly single till my mid-30s, and infertile for years after my marriage, I can identify with both. We may know intellectually that neither a loving husband nor childbearing is the whole point of life; but we still feel that way when we are longing for them!

I had the support of close women friends; Rachel and Leah had no sisterly sharing, only a bitter contest. No wonder their children continued the family tradition of conflict when they made Joseph, the favourite, 'disappear' (Genesis 37:12–36).

PRAYER

Lord, I often long so much for what I don't have that I forget to thank you for what I have. Help me to see your hand in all of life, not just when things go the way I want.

DINAH

GENESIS 34:1–7 (ABRIDGED)

Now Dinah the daughter of Leah... went out to visit the women of the region. When Shechem son of Hamor the Hivite, prince of the region, saw her, he seized her and lay with her by force. And his soul was drawn to Dinah daughter of Jacob; he loved the girl, and spoke tenderly to her. So Shechem spoke to his father Hamor, saying, 'Get me this girl to be my wife.'

Now Jacob heard that Shechem had defiled his daughter Dinah; but his sons were with his cattle in the field, so Jacob held his peace until they came. And Hamor the father of Shechem went out to Jacob to speak with him, just as the sons of Jacob came in from the field. When they heard of it, the men were indignant and very angry, because he had committed an outrage in Israel by lying with Jacob's daughter, for such a thing ought not to be done.

Twelve sons and one solitary daughter—I wonder how they regarded her? Perhaps with a mixture of protectiveness and patronizing: 'You're only a girl, you can't join in with us.' We don't know why she was visiting 'the women of the region', but it would be understandable if she longed for some female companionship!

Dinah was about 14, calculating from her brother Joseph's age (37:2). It was a marriageable age in that society, and in later law (see Deuteronomy 22:28–29) Shechem's 'compensation' would be perfectly acceptable. But this is a time before formalized laws, when the measured retribution of 'an eye for an eye' has not yet been imposed. Dinah's mob of brothers, pretending at first to accept the offer, launch into bloody revenge that sours their relations with all their neighbours. Shechem's one act of violence escalates into hundreds.

And what of the girl at the centre of it all? Try to imagine her confusion and distress: attacked one minute, courted the next; promised in marriage, then snatched away. No rape crisis centre for her, no counselling, no asking how she felt about her fate. Would she have been willing to marry Shechem? Did she revel in the destruction of his clan? We cannot know. She is family property that has been damaged, and the family exacts its price.

REFLECTION

Think of ways in which law protects the vulnerable in your society. Do you think it does so sufficiently in practice? Pray for law-makers and law courts, that they may truly defend the weak.

---- 32 ----

SHIPHRAH AND PUAH

EXODUS 1:15–20

The king of Egypt said to the Hebrew midwives, one of whom was named Shiphrah and the other Puah, 'When you act as midwives to the Hebrew women, and see them on the birthstool, if it is a boy kill him; but if it is a girl, she shall live.' But the midwives feared God; they did not do as the king of Egypt commanded them, but they let the boys live. So the king of Egypt summoned the midwives and said to them, 'Why have you done this, and allowed the boys to live?' The midwives said to Pharaoh, 'Because the Hebrew women are not like the Egyptian women; for they are vigorous and give birth before the midwife comes to them.' So God dealt well with the midwives; and the people multiplied and became very strong.

In the second-century *Epistle to Diognetus*, the author describes what is different about Christians. It is not, he says, 'a matter of nationality, or language, or customs. Christians do not live apart in separate cities... speak any special dialect, nor practise any eccentric way of life... Like other people, they marry and beget children, though they do not expose their infants.' What's this about exposing infants? In the culture of the day, and in many since, unwanted (usually female) babies were simply left in wasteland to die. Still, today, in some countries disabled children are dumped in orphanages, or excess mouths are sent to beg their bread on the streets; and in the West unwanted pregnancies are simply terminated.

In Pharaoh's Egypt it was, for different reasons, the boys who were unwanted. But the midwives 'feared God'. We have seen plenty of oppression in our readings in Genesis; Exodus opens with a stirring note of liberation. Shiphrah and Puah are the first practitioners of civil disobedience, direct action to undermine the power of the tyrant. While they do not knuckle under, neither do they recklessly seek martyrdom: their 'white lie' allows them to go on serving their growing community.

Standing up against evil needs strategy and it needs community. Shiprah and Puah act together and they act creatively. They are 'wise as serpents, and innocent as doves' (Matthew 10:16).

PRAYER

Are you, or is your church, involved in protecting the weak and opposing oppression? Do you know of others who are? Pray for them to have the qualities they need: wisdom, courage and solidarity in the fight.

33

DEBORAH

JUDGES 4:1–8 (ABRIDGED)

The Israelites again did what was evil in the sight of the Lord, after Ehud died. So the Lord sold them into the hand of King Jabin of Canaan, who reigned in Hazor; the commander of his army was Sisera... Then the Israelites cried out to the Lord for help; for he had nine hundred chariots of iron, and had oppressed the Israelites cruelly for twenty years.

At that time Deborah, a prophetess, wife of Lappidoth, was judging Israel. She used to sit under the palm of Deborah... and the Israelites came up to her for judgment. She sent and summoned Barak... and said to him, 'The Lord, the God of Israel, commands you, "Go, take position at Mount Tabor, bringing ten thousand from the tribe of Naphtali and the tribe of Zebulun. I will draw out Sisera, the general of Jabin's army, to meet you by the Wadi Kishon with his chariots and his troops; and I will give him into your hand."' Barak said to her, 'If you will go with me, I will go; but if you will not go with me, I will not go.'

Two of the first judges God provided for his people were a left-handed man (Ehud, Judges 3:15) and a woman. But the remarkable thing about Deborah's leadership is that the Bible does not remark on it. It is related as if a female supreme judge was quite normal.

Deborah is quite a leader, for General Barak refuses to go into battle without her moral support. She displays both spiritual and managerial gifts—and, judging by chapter 5, she is no mean poet!

Unlike some women in leadership, she also celebrates the gifts of other women: 'Most blessed of women be Jael... She put her hand to the tent peg... she struck Sisera a blow... there he fell dead' (5:24, 26–27). And the victory poem goes on to imagine Sisera's mother watching from her window for him, fancying he is dividing the spoil: 'a girl or two for every man' (v. 30). Is this an unfeminine glorification of violence? Or is it a woman's ability to see how other women are affected?

Perhaps Deborah's greatest gift is to acknowledge the work of the whole community: 'When the people offer themselves willingly— bless the Lord!' (5:2) . Deborah, Barak, Jael—as a sermon preached in my church said, 'leadership is plural'.

REFLECTION

'She put her hand to the tent peg…' What could be achieved if women put their hands to 'beating swords into ploughshares' (see Isaiah 2:4)?

34

JEPHTHAH'S DAUGHTER

JUDGES 11:29–35 (ABRIDGED)

The spirit of the Lord came upon Jephthah, and he passed through Gilead and Manasseh... and from Mizpah of Gilead he passed on to the Ammonites. And Jephthah made a vow to the Lord, and said, 'If you will give the Ammonites into my hand, then whoever comes out of the doors of my house to meet me, when I return victorious from the Ammonites, shall be the Lord's, to be offered up by me as a burnt offering.' So Jephthah crossed over to the Ammonites to fight against them; and the Lord gave them into his hand...

Then Jephthah came to his home at Mizpah; and there was his daughter coming out to meet him with timbrels and with dancing. She was his only child; he had no son or daughter except her. When he saw her, he tore his clothes, and said, 'Alas, my daughter! You have brought me very low; you have become the cause of great trouble to me.'

'A woman's place is in the wrong', goes a feminist saying. Jephthah, another of those unlikely judges that God chose—a prostitute's son, rejected by his half-brothers, living as an outlaw—has made a thoughtless, desperate promise. But whom does he blame for the outcome? The victim.

His daughter's restrained response has the tone of a Greek tragedy: 'My father, if you have opened your mouth to the Lord, do to me according to what has gone out of your mouth... Let this thing be done for me: Grant me two months, so that I may go and wander on the mountains, and bewail my virginity, my companions and I' (vv. 36–37).

What was she bewailing? The fact that through her father's self-centredness, she would never fulfil her destiny as a woman in that society. Her situation may seem very far from ours, lost in the mists of a primitive culture. But how many of us have been kept from wholeness by the 'care-lessness' of others—whether parents, teachers, employers or church leaders? Every day, people are sacrificed to political, military, economic or personal ends. Sacrificing others is something that any of us might be guilty of; and many of us have been the sacrifice.

PRAYER

'Every year the daughters of Israel would go out to lament the daughter of Jephthah' (v. 40). Choose a group of people who you feel have been 'sacrificed', and find a way to lament them, perhaps by writing a prayer.

35

SAMSON'S WIFE

JUDGES 14:1–2, 10–17 (ABRIDGED)

Once Samson went down to Timnah, and at Timnah he saw a Philistine woman. Then he came up, and told his father and mother, 'I saw a Philistine woman at Timnah; now get her for me as my wife.' ...

His father went down to the woman, and Samson made a feast there as the young men were accustomed to do... Samson said to them, 'Let me now put a riddle to you...' On the fourth day they said to Samson's wife, 'Coax your husband to explain the riddle to us, or we will burn you and your father's house with fire...' So Samson's wife wept before him, saying, 'You hate me; you do not really love me. You have asked a riddle of my people, but you have not explained it to me.' He said to her, 'Look, I have not told my father or my mother. Why should I tell you?' She wept before him the seven days that their feast lasted; and because she nagged him, on the seventh day he told her.

It could come from any modern *Rambo*-style film. Muscle man fancies one of the enemy's women, demands her and defies all his parents' opposition. On his way to see her, he kills a lion. Coming back to fetch her, he sees the lion's carcass with a bees' nest in it, and at the wedding feast he makes it into a puzzle to tease her friends. When they have threatened his bride into cajoling the answer from him, Samson's violence is out of all proportion. And his wife is passed on to his best man. (Read the whole chapter to get the full story.)

Throughout the sorry tale, one note re-echoes: 'he did not tell them'. The strong silent hero is just that—silent. It is only after deciding he 'must have' the girl that he bothers to talk to her.

This girl, caught in a tribal conflict, is a forerunner of the more famous Delilah. I have some sympathy with both of them. When men won't communicate, what can women do but manipulate?

Samson treats women as playthings; they use tears to get the better of him. It is all very childish, and very familiar. And it's a long way from the Christian model of marriage: 'each of you should love his wife as himself, and a wife should respect her husband' (Ephesians 5:33).

REFLECTION

'A man leaves his father and his mother and cleaves to his wife' (Genesis 2:24, RSV). Think about what 'leaving' and 'cleaving' really mean.

36

THE LEVITE'S CONCUBINE

JUDGES 19:22–30 (ABRIDGED)

While they were enjoying themselves, the men of the city, a depraved lot, surrounded the house, and... said to the old man... 'Bring out the man who came into your house, so that we may have intercourse with him.' And the man, the master of the house, went out to them and said to them, 'No, my brothers, do not act so wickedly... Here are my virgin daughter and his concubine... Ravish them and do whatever you want to them...' But the men would not listen to him. So the man seized his concubine and put her out to them. They wantonly raped her, and abused her all through the night until the morning.... In the morning her master got up, opened the doors of the house, and... there was his concubine lying at the door of the house... 'Get up,' he said to her, 'we are going.' But there was no answer... When he had entered his house, he took a knife, and... cut her into twelve pieces... and sent her throughout all the territory of Israel. Then he commanded the men whom he sent, saying, 'Thus shall you say to all the Israelites, "Has such a thing ever happened since the day that the Israelites came up from the land of Egypt until this day? Consider it, take counsel, and speak out."'

Recently an Austrian tourist was raped in London by a gang of teenagers. Her husband's reaction seems to have been mainly anger with her. But, as this account shows, there never have been 'good old days' when such things did not happen. This has to be the nastiest story in the whole Bible. Why read it, then? Because it is there; because it happened.

'In those days,' we are reminded at the beginning of the chapter, 'there was no king in Israel', and, as Judges repeats frequently, each man did as he liked. The men of Gibeah are not looking for a 'meaningful relationship', either hetero- or homosexual. They lust for sensation, and people are their raw material.

But are the Levite or his host much better? In the Middle East at that time, the law of hospitality was paramount. In honouring it, it seems, women were dispensable. The Levite's outrage leads to a bloody war—but it did not stop him surrendering his concubine to begin with.

REFLECTION

When the vulnerable are abused and their 'protectors' compound the damage, 'Consider it, take counsel, and speak out' (v. 30).

A COLOURFUL STORY

In the kingless land of Inequalia lived two varieties of people: the Reds and the Greens. To the casual observer there seemed to be little difference between them, apart from their colour, and the main purpose of this difference appeared to be that one adult of each colour was required to reproduce the species, so that it was rather useful to be able to distinguish them from each other.

However, anyone who studied the Inequalian culture closely would soon discover that the daily lives of Reds and Greens were vastly different. To begin with, they were expected to wear different clothes (although it was perfectly easy to tell them apart by their colour), and anyone who blurred this distinction would incur severe disapproval. The clothing rules were actually quite irksome, as the garments approved for Reds were generally much more comfortable and hard-wearing than those allotted to Greens—even though many Greens did far more demanding physical work than Reds. But Greens, so the accepted wisdom ran, should dress decoratively to please Reds, not practically to please themselves.

These dress customs were merely the outward show of a much deeper divide. In fact, there was virtually no area of life in which the two groups were not educated and regulated into being almost the exact opposite of each other. Usually this was justified on the basis of what were called 'natural roles'. Reds, it was argued, stood out, by their colour, from the landscape. They were therefore clearly meant to be bold, assertive, dynamic, and to take on leadership functions. Greens, on the other hand, merged into the grassy background. They were obviously meant to be quiet, unassuming, to take the attitude of followers and defer to the judgment of the Reds, whose needs they were ideally suited to serve.

At the same time as insisting that these 'natural roles' were inborn and eternal, the Inequalian philosophers (who were all Red) also reacted with horror to any attempt to relax the network of rules and customs that maintained the roles—for fear that if these barriers were broken, the distinction between Reds and Greens would be destroyed. They seemed to see no contradiction at all in their arguments; but then they were, of course, a primitive people.

From their very earliest years, Reds and Greens were trained to conform to their 'natural roles'. They were encouraged to differ in personality, interests, activities and friendships. Woe betide any youthful Red who displayed aptitudes or concerns not considered colour-appropriate: friends' taunts of 'Greenie!' would soon put a stop to that. Similarly, any adolescent Green would be mortified to be considered 'Reddish', for although redness was universally accepted to be the better state, it was not one to which a Green should aspire.

As the young Inequalians grew up, their colour would dictate their career, regardless of what talents they showed. Reds were directed towards jobs that involved initiative, risk and authority, such as hunting the blue mammoth, whose tongue was a particular delicacy, or being elected master of the monthly 'roaring', at which issues of justice were decided by means of a shouting match.

Greens, meanwhile, were encouraged to take on domestic tasks such as rearing the young and mucking out the cave. These jobs were considered 'too green' (which was another way of saying 'too insignificant') for Reds to concern themselves with.

Very occasionally, by sheer determination, a Green might manage to acquire training in a red area of work, such as poison-dart spitting or the underwater squid race that was the national sport—or even the performance of the spiritual mysteries. But it was very unlikely that any opportunities would be provided for a Green to exercise these skills. Greens should stick to what they were best at, was the general opinion. The fact that some Greens were better at traditional red tasks than at their own green ones was resolutely ignored.

The relation of these social structures to the Inequalians' religion was a complex one. Long ago in prehistory, the Inequalians had deduced that their land was far too beautiful and rich to have happened by accident, and that it must therefore have a Creator. As redness was a desirable quality that gave people status and power, it was usually thought that the Creator must be Red. Reds were made in the Creator's image; and Greens, though made by the same hand, were but a pale imitation.

The philosophers also pointed out, however, that the land was beautiful and rich, but flawed and dogged by a constant battle for survival. Many of its inhabitants lived on infertile land, where they could hardly grow enough of the common purple rootwort to eat, while others, more fortunate, dined in luxury on smoked blue mammoth tongue. All this suggested that some catastrophic event had occurred, now lost in the mists of time, which had twisted and marred the land.

Some dissidents took this doctrine of the Great Catastrophe further. Before it, they said, the land had been called Equalia, and Reds and Greens had ruled it jointly, exercising the gifts the Creator had given them with no restrictions based on colours. This view, however, was pooh-poohed by the Guardians of the Mysteries (who, again, were all Reds). The distinction between the colours, they said, were unchangeable and had been ordained by the Creator from all time. If Greens were meant to be noticed, would they have been created green? And in any case, it was the inbuilt frailty of the Greens that had brought about the Great Catastrophe in the first place. Did the dissidents not know the story of the First Wicked Green, who disobeyed the Creator and hid in the grass, hoping not to be found out?

The Guardians also told how, hundreds of years before, a Red had been born who was so different from all other Inequalians, so free from all known flaws and cruelties, that the people of that time concluded that this had to be the Creator in person, disguised as a mortal and visiting the land to usher in the Great Reversal, by which the effects of the Great Catastrophe were eventually to be undone. Although all this had happened so long ago, it was believed that the 'Redchild' was still mysteriously present in the person of the 'Holy

Redness', an invisible being through whom the Creator would occasionally issue decrees.

But when rebellious Greens pleaded for greater freedom to express themselves, the Guardians would always make much of the fact that the Creator had appeared as a Red. They, as Reds, were the natural representatives of a Red Creator, who visited the land as Redchild and communicated through the Holy Redness. How could a Green, who was so much more limited, so ignorant of all but young-rearing and cave mucking-out, possibly pass on the teachings of Redchild or faithfully transmit the decrees of the Holy Redness?

To the dedicated student of lost primitive peoples, the history of Inequalia is indeed a fruitful field. I could spend many hours unfolding to you their strange colour-based customs. But they were long ago and far away, and nothing to do with our own land. After all, we don't arrange things so muddleheadedly ourselves, do we?

HARD TIMES

'How do you know God cares for you?' asked the teacher of the young teens at our church. 'Because really bad things don't happen to us,' came the answer. She groaned inwardly. Should she tell them now, or wait until life made them sadder and wiser? What if they still thought the same at 30?

This section is about what we do when the bad things do happen, because, for sure, they will. A few years ago, I went to a college reunion, and met again, after 24 years, a friend I'd lost touch with. She barely looked a day older than when we graduated: she was tanned, slim and full of life. She had been happily married for over 20 years, had two clever children about to go to college, was managing two careers as a law lecturer and a self-taught nutritionist, and, to cap it all, the family owned a holiday home in France.

I was positively green with envy as I dwelt on the fact that I hadn't married till I was 36, had my son at 41 and was still struggling to get him into an appropriate infant school for his special needs. A few years later, however, I went back to another reunion, having failed to keep in touch with my friend in between. Sure enough, she was there again. But she looked rather older and somewhat subdued. In the course of the weekend, it emerged that two years earlier, her 22-year-old daughter, recently graduated with a first, had been killed in a car crash. I vowed I would never envy anyone again.

There is an old Jewish story about a mother who loses her son and complains bitterly to God. Eventually, tired of her complaints, God says, 'I will give you your son back, as soon as you can find a household in which there has been no tragedy.' So she goes from house to house, inquiring as to each one's history. After months, she returns to the throne of God. God knows at once, from her expression, that her quest has been in vain. There is no such household.

That being the case, I thank God that from Job to Joel, the Bible is full of tragic stories and people's response to them. This is no 'health and wealth' book, but one full of consolation and wisdom for the times when everything falls apart.

PSALMS 73–89: SAVE US, GOD!

Most of what I know about God, I have learned from being a parent. My understanding of these psalms is no exception. The other day, my son had a severe tantrum over something quite trivial. It was clearly important to him, even if it didn't seem so to me! I did my best to comfort and calm him down, but his tears were not going to make me give in to his request. (I did eventually make a concession!) Still, I would rather he continue to bring his distress, and his demands, to me, than go off and express them to a stranger—or keep them in and end up expressing them in more destructive ways.

Perhaps God, as our father (and mother?) feels the same. Maybe God would rather hear our complaints, our accusations, even our shouts of rebellion, than hear nothing from us. This group of psalms (the third of five 'books') is mostly composed of what my husband would call 'whingeing psalms'. More politely, they are known as psalms of lament. The psalmist, of course, is going to God with more serious issues than 'I want that brand of crisps and no other'. He is recording real personal and national pain, which God doesn't seem to be addressing.

The Christian church is just beginning to wake up to this lost tradition of lament. It is one of the necessary stages in coming to terms with difficult events or circumstances in our life, and we miss it out at our peril.

When I wrote the notes that follow, we as a family were going through an exceptionally difficult period. When you're in the middle of suffering, it seems as if it will never get any better. Yet just as I started to write, after months of frustration, we got several pieces of good news, and then four really encouraging letters arrived from readers of previous notes. Suddenly it was easier to praise God! However, many of these psalms praise God even in the midst of crisis. That's something I've still got to learn.

The book of Psalms is often called 'the Old Testament in miniature'. As such, I believe it should be approached, like the rest of the Old Testament, only through the 'lens' of Jesus and the redemption he brings. So I have tried to make a link to Jesus each day, and because psalms are ultimately prayers, on several days I have ended with a line from Jesus' own prayer.

37

WHY SO UNFAIR?

PSALM 73:1–5, 13–14, 16–17

Truly God is good to the upright, to those who are pure in heart. But as for me, my feet had almost stumbled; my steps had nearly slipped. For I was envious of the arrogant; I saw the prosperity of the wicked. For they have no pain; their bodies are sound and sleek. They are not in trouble as others are; they are not plagued like other people...

All in vain I have kept my heart clean and washed my hands in innocence. For all day long I have been plagued, and am punished every morning...

But when I thought how to understand this, it seemed to me a wearisome task, until I went into the sanctuary of God; then I perceived their end.

In the Victorian girls' stories that I read as a child, the heroine always struggles with a 'besetting sin'—a character flaw such as vanity or pride. I know exactly what my 'besetting sin' is: it's envy. Everyone has an easier life, more co-operative children, a better-tempered husband, a nicer and cleaner house, than I do.

My envy, however, pales into insignificance beside the 'global envy' from which the psalmist suffers here. It's all so *unfair*—why do some people seem to have no troubles at all, while often the very best people stumble from disaster to disaster?

As a child, after a row with my mother, I would run out of the house to the nearby railway halt, where there was a footbridge across the tracks. Somehow, standing on the bridge and looking down calmed me and put everything into perspective.

British Rail pulled my bridge down, but the psalmist has a better way of 'seeing from above': he goes into the temple to pray. For us, this might mean sitting alone with a Bible or a candle to meditate;

or visiting a Christian friend, or going to church.

Why some people prosper and others don't is the great mystery of life. Pretending that God will smooth every path for us can only end in disappointment. Jesus called us to 'take up your cross' (Matthew 16:24); that hardly sounds like an easy life!

REFLECTION

'He did not say, "You will not be assailed, you will not be belaboured, you will not be disquieted", but he said, "You will not be overcome"' (Julian of Norwich). Let this inspire your worship.

38

THE BROKEN SHEEPFOLD

PSALM 74:1–4, 9–10a

O God, why do you cast us off for ever? Why does your anger smoke against the sheep of your pasture? Remember your congregation, which you acquired long ago, which you redeemed to be the tribe of your heritage. Remember Mount Zion, where you came to dwell. Direct your steps to the perpetual ruins; the enemy has destroyed everything in the sanctuary. Your foes have roared within your holy place; they set up their emblems there…

We do not see our emblems; there is no longer any prophet, and there is no one among us who knows how long. How long, O God…?

Ever since the beginning of the charismatic movement, there have been those who came out with convincing-sounding prophecies predicting that there would be 'revival' in such-and-such a year. Yet those years have passed, and the church in Europe has continued to decline.

When there seem to be so few who follow Jesus wholeheartedly and the church is classed as a 'leisure activity', when Christians feel beleaguered and isolated and we see the world wandering in darkness 'like sheep without a shepherd' (Matthew 9:36), it is tempting to have a neat answer to 'How long, O God?' (v. 10).

For the ancient Israelites it was more so, as national disaster and religious disaster were the same thing. This psalm was clearly a response to enemy invasion, probably by Babylon (imagine that Hitler had succeeded in invading Britain). The worst thing is that the invader has desecrated the temple and set up pagan military symbols there.

In the Western world, the signs of God's kingdom seem few, and signs of consumerism, cynicism and chaotic lives are everywhere. How long until the kingdom comes? How long till God makes 'all things new' (Revelation 21:5)? Maybe not until we Christians are fit for the new world.

The only answer is in verse 12: 'Yet God my King is from of old, working salvation in the earth.' The psalmist contemplates God's 'miracles' of creation: the sea, the gushing rivers, the sun and moon, the seasons. Will this creative God not save God's 'little flock'—and more, God's world? We don't need to know when, just that the day will come. Meanwhile, 'I am the good shepherd. I know my own' (John 10:14).

PRAYER

Our Father in heaven, hallowed be your name.

----- 39 -----

GOD ON A MISSION

PSALM 75:1–3, 76:1–6 (ABRIDGED)

We give thanks to you, O God; we give thanks; your name is near. People tell of your wondrous deeds. At the set time that I appoint I will judge with equity. When the earth totters, with all its inhabitants, it is I who keep its pillars steady...

In Judah God is known, his name is great in Israel... There he broke the flashing arrows, the shield, the sword, and the weapons of war... The stout-hearted were stripped of their spoil; they sank into sleep; none of the troops was able to lift a hand. At your rebuke, O God of Jacob, both rider and horse lay stunned.

Have you ever watched a mother swooping in to rescue her child from a potentially dangerous situation? Have you seen (or experienced) that powerful blend of anger and passionate love?

That mixture of fury and concern is what these two psalms bring to mind for me. They have been linked to the rescue of Jerusalem from the Assyrian invasion that destroyed the northern kingdom in the eighth century BC. Psalm 75 has a picture of God holding 'a cup with foaming wine, well mixed; he will pour a draught from it, and all the wicked of the earth shall drain it down to the dregs' (v. 8). This picture of God's judgment as a 'poisoned chalice' is common in the Old Testament. Psalm 76:7 portrays God as 'awesome!' and asks, 'Who can stand before you when once your anger is roused?'

When we think of 'the wrath of God' as described, for instance, in Romans 1, we may imagine a kind of cold, detached, head-masterly anger (apologies to any headmasters reading this)—a sort of 'This hurts me more that it hurts you' statement that always fails to convince. I believe, however, that God's anger, against evil and in defence of God's people, is a passionate, swooping-down sort of anger, which really does hurt God more than us.

That is the sort of God I see in these psalms—'on a mission', storming in to rescue the beloved people. It is no accident that we call Jesus' death 'the passion': God is passionate about people, passionate for justice.

PRAYER

Your kingdom come, your will be done.

── 40 ──

TEACH YOUR CHILDREN WELL

PSALM 78:1–5

Give ear, O my people, to my teaching; incline your ears to the words of my mouth. I will open my mouth in a parable; I will utter dark sayings from of old, things that we have heard and known, that our ancestors have told us. We will not hide them from their children; we will tell to the coming generation the glorious deeds of the Lord, and his might, and the wonders that he has done. He established a decree in Jacob, and appointed a law in Israel, which he commanded our ancestors to teach to their children.

Before I was a mother, I was sceptical about 'bringing up children as Christians'. I had seen too many people rebel against a church up-bringing, and felt that my secular background hadn't prevented me from finding God (or God from finding me!)

Now I'm not so sure. The fact is, life with God is so central to Ed and me that we could not possibly keep our son from it. He is surrounded by people who follow Jesus, and something must rub off on him. I only hope it will be the best bits, and not the ones where we've distorted God's message!

This long psalm takes us through Israel's entire history: the giving of the law, the pillars of cloud and fire in the wilderness, water from the rock, manna from heaven, the feast of quails, and then a 'flashback' to the plagues in Egypt. It is clearly a teaching psalm, perhaps recited in worship as a 'beginner's guide' to God's saving of the chosen people.

It also goes into some detail about the people's frequent rebellions—a warning, perhaps, to the attentive listener not to repeat their mistakes? 'Yet he', the writer points out, 'being compassionate,

111

forgave their iniquity, and did not destroy them; often he restrained his anger, and did not stir up all his wrath' (v. 38).

We too are bound to tell our children the story of how God has loved and blessed us. Let's make sure we don't only tell the bits where we got it right. It is about God's goodness, not ours: 'no one is good but God alone' (Mark 10:18).

REFLECTION

'Whoever welcomes one such child in my name welcomes me, and whoever welcomes me welcomes not me but the one who sent me' (Mark 9:37).

41

GOD'S PR OFFICE

PSALM 79:1–4, 8b–10a

O God, the nations have come into your inheritance; they have defiled your holy temple; they have laid Jerusalem in ruins. They have given the bodies of your servants to the birds of the air for food, the flesh of your faithful to the wild animals of the earth. They have poured out their blood like water all around Jerusalem, and there was no one to bury them. We have become a taunt to our neighbours, mocked and derided by those around us...

Let your compassion come speedily to meet us, for we are brought very low. Help us, O God of our salvation, for the glory of your name; deliver us, and forgive our sins, for your name's sake. Why should the nations say, 'Where is their God?'

Nowadays every large organization has to have a public relations office. Often, however, that office is accused of 'spin': presenting the organization in the best possible light, regardless of how true it is.

God's 'PR office', as presented in this psalm, is different. The psalmist wants people to think well of God, but this is not a case of covering up God's failures; it is a desire for the truth about God's goodness to come out. He believes that God is good, but is having a hard time convincing the sceptical. Why would a good God have allowed God's chosen people to be overrun by invaders, their holy place destroyed, their city in ruins, unburied bodies lying everywhere?

Many a country and many an individual could echo this lament. The explanations offered—such as 'God is punishing us for our sins' or 'If God seems far away, who moved?'—are always inadequate. In these circumstances, if we want to hold on to our faith, there is only one thing to do: cry out to God in the darkness, trusting that our past experiences of grace were not an illusion, that God will return 'like the spring rains that water the earth' (Hosea 6:3).

We may get tied up about whether we are 'a good witness', but ultimately God's reputation does not depend on us, it depends on God. The best PR for God is Jesus.

PRAYER

Give us today our daily bread!

42

THE TRAMPLED VINE

PSALM 80:8–14

You brought a vine out of Egypt; you drove out the nations and planted it. You cleared the ground for it; it took deep root and filled the land. The mountains were covered with its shade, the mighty cedars with its branches; it sent out its branches to the sea, and its shoots to the River. Why then have you broken down its walls, so that all who pass along the way pluck its fruit? The boar from the forest ravages it, and all that move in the field feed on it. Turn again, O God of hosts; look down from heaven, and see; have regard for this vine.

During a reflection process in my church, we were reading books on church growth and alternative ways of being church. The ones I read had plenty of diagnoses as to why the church in Europe is in decline, but so far I've seen few solutions. Yet churches are flourishing in Latin America, Africa, the Far East. Could it be that it's just not our turn?

This psalm is a lament for the northern kingdom of Israel, utterly destroyed by Assyria. In Psalm 74 we saw God's people as a sheep-fold with broken-down walls; here they are a vine trampled by wild animals. Jesus takes both these common Old Testament images and applies them to himself: 'I am the good shepherd' (John 10:11); 'I am the true vine' (John 15:1). By this he identifies himself with God, the keeper of the sheepfold, and with God's people, the vine that God tends.

No single nation is 'God's people' now, but Jesus' use of these images gives us licence to use this psalm in praying for the restoration of Jesus' body, the Church. We must remember, however, that the northern kingdom was never restored, until modern Israel was given parts of it. We may long for the power that the Church had in the past, but God is more likely to say 'I am about to do a new thing' (Isaiah 43:19); and that new thing may spring up where we least expect it. Just like the vine, the purpose of God's people is not to rule the world, but to bless it.

PRAYER

'Restore us, O God; let your face shine, that we may be saved' (Psalm 80:3, 7, 19).

43

GOD ANSWERS BACK

PSALM 81:8–16 (ABRIDGED)

Hear, O my people, while I admonish you; O Israel, if you would but listen to me! There shall be no strange god among you; you shall not bow down to a foreign god. I am the Lord your God, who brought you up out of the land of Egypt... But my people did not listen to my voice; Israel would not submit to me. So I gave them over to their stubborn hearts, to follow their own counsels. O that my people would listen to me, that Israel would walk in my ways! ... I would feed you with the finest of the wheat, and with honey from the rock I would satisfy you.

C.S. Lewis, in *Miracles*, describes encountering God as holding on to the end of a line (a fishing line, maybe), suddenly feeling a twitch from the other end and exclaiming in terror, 'It's alive!' This psalm is one of those twitches. You don't have to imagine the psalmist taking dictation from God; the writer is probably imagining what God would say, but imagining on the basis of experience.

We have heard, in other psalms, a lot of complaining about God's absence. Here God reminds us of the times of presence: 'I relieved your shoulder of the burden; your hands were freed from the basket. In distress you called, and I rescued you; I answered you in the secret place of thunder' (vv. 6–7). This is a message to the whole people of Israel, calling them to remember how God rescued them from slavery. But there are less welcome reminders too: 'But my people did not listen...' (v. 11). Forgetfulness and unfaithfulness are the bad habits of God's people—and not only in the Old Testament!

Are we to understand that every time we suffer, it is evidence of God punishing us? Jesus himself denied that, when people asked him about a notorious disaster, the collapse of the tower at Siloam (Luke 13:4). Those who were killed, he said, were no better or worse than others—we all need to repent.

This psalm, however, is more than a rebuke or a warning; it is an invitation: 'I would feed you...' (v. 16). It is God's yearning for us, not God's irritation with us, that wins out here.

REFLECTION

When you pray, what kind of answer are you expecting?

44

JUDGING THE JUDGES

PSALM 82:1–4

God has taken his place in the divine council; in the midst of the gods he holds judgment: 'How long will you judge unjustly and show partiality to the wicked? Give justice to the weak and the orphan; maintain the right of the lowly and the destitute. Rescue the weak and the needy; deliver them from the hand of the wicked.'

As I write, we have just had a major public inquiry in the United Kingdom, with another to come soon. Already people are criticizing the judge who conducted the first, and alleging that he was biased. Yet our judicial system is at least free from corruption; in many others, judges are routinely bribed, and justice for the poor and powerless is totally unavailable. Who will judge the judges?

The idea of God's 'divine council', a kind of 'parliament of the gods', is a very ancient one, whose best-known expression is at the start of Job. Later writers saw the other 'gods' as just figments of the imagination: 'Can mortals make for themselves gods? Such are no gods!' (Jeremiah 16:20).

Some commentators, however, think that God here is addressing human judges, who have 'god-like' power. Either way, the responsibility of these 'assistants to God' is to do God's work of administering justice and defending the poor. If those in power end up perpetuating inequality and defending the rich, they themselves will come under judgment.

Jesus quotes this psalm in John 10:34: 'Is it not written in your law, "I said, you are gods"?' He uses it to justify referring to God as his father, which the religious leaders call blasphemy. Every human being, he seems to be saying, is potentially godlike—after all, we are made in God's image. But, 'Let the same mind be in you that was in Christ Jesus, who, though he was in the form of God, did not regard equality with God as something to be exploited, but emptied himself, taking the form of a slave, being born in human likeness' (Philippians 2:5–7). Our godlikeness is best expressed in Christlike service, not in a desire for God's power.

PRAYER

'Forgive us our sins'. Pray this not just for yourself but for the world.

---- 45 ----

VISITING GOD

PSALM 84:1–4

How lovely is your dwelling place, O Lord of hosts! My soul longs, indeed it faints for the courts of the Lord; my heart and my flesh sing for joy to the living God. Even the sparrow finds a home, and the swallow a nest for herself, where she may lay her young, at your altars, O Lord of hosts, my King and my God. Happy are those who live in your house, ever singing your praise.

Do you have a special place? Somewhere you go regularly on retreat, or a holiday location? Or is it perhaps a special group of people among whom you instantly feel relaxed and at home?

I've always been more of a 'places' person; indeed, it was only when I became a parent that I began to take photographs of people rather than places. So this psalm resonates deeply with me; it takes me to a place where God seems particularly close, a 'thin place' as the Celtic Christians called it.

Psalm 84 could be a sequel to Psalm 73: it is only in the temple that the writer finds a sense of peace about the inequalities and sufferings of the world. Is church, for us, a place like this? Or is it full of tensions, annoyances, conflicts?

For followers of Jesus, the gathered people of God take the place of the temple. We need to find our security and sanity among those 'in whose heart are the highways to Zion' (v. 5). If we don't find it there, we may need, prayerfully and gently, to seek change in our church, or move to another one. But the first step is to make sure that those highways are in our own heart!

I'm still a person who inclines to hidden-away places; but, having found a church where I can belong wholeheartedly, I'm learning to find the presence of God among God's people. There are no sparrows or swallows there—the roof is undamaged!—but I hope we are 'breeding' a people who will care for God's earth. And I hope lots of human 'lost birds' can find a nest among us, too.

REFLECTION

'As they go through the valley of Baca they make it a place of springs; the early rain also covers it with pools' (v. 6). Recall the 'desert places' of your own life and try to identify the 'springs'.

46

AGAIN, AGAIN!

PSALM 85:1–4, 8–11 (ABRIDGED)

Lord, you were favourable to your land; you restored the fortunes of Jacob. You forgave the iniquity of your people; you pardoned all their sin... Restore us again, O God of our salvation, and put away your indignation toward us... Let me hear what God the Lord will speak, for he will speak peace to his people, to his faithful, to those who turn to him in their hearts... Steadfast love and faithfulness will meet; righteousness and peace will kiss each other. Faithfulness will spring up from the ground, and righteousness will look down from the sky.

In the much-maligned but also much-loved *Teletubbies* children's television show, the four characters, after watching a short video, cry, 'Again, again!' Children love to have experiences repeated; they are testing the world to see if what happened once will happen again. Will Daddy catch me this time? Of course Daddy always does. So gradually they learn that objects (and people) will always fall, but also that Daddy is trustworthy.

The people of Israel, in this psalm, are behaving in a similar way. 'God saved us in the past; we tell the story again at every Passover. But will God save us from this new, unexpected trial?'

I know how they felt. Time and again, when life gets hard, I begin to doubt whether God is in control of my life or even interested in it. Am I going to be abandoned to my fate? Will depression, tiredness, the stress of city life, the battles of parenting, unhelpful authorities or marital misunderstandings overcome me? Or will God send help?

Time and again—just in time, just enough—God does step in

123

with surprising blessings. Yet next time, I know, I will still doubt God's goodness or ability to save me.

This psalm deals with that recurrent doubt by looking to God's help in the past: God has been generous and merciful. It also looks to the future: a time where justice and peace will, in a lovely phrase, 'kiss each other'. In Christ our hope is even clearer: 'that the creation itself will be set free from its bondage to decay and will obtain the freedom of the glory of the children of God' (Romans 8:21).

REFLECTION

'Rejoice in hope, be patient in suffering, persevere in prayer' (Romans 12:12).

47

SHOW ME

PSALM 86:1–2, 14–17 (ABRIDGED)

Incline your ear, O Lord, and answer me, for I am poor and needy. Preserve my life, for I am devoted to you; save your servant who trusts in you. You are my God...

O God, the insolent rise up against me; a band of ruffians seeks my life, and they do not set you before them. But you, O Lord, are a God merciful and gracious, slow to anger and abounding in steadfast love and faithfulness... Show me a sign of your favour, so that those who hate me may see it and be put to shame, because you, Lord, have helped me and comforted me.

Do I detect a note of manipulation here? The psalmist could be saying something like, 'After all I've done for you, God, it's time you did something for me.' He even invokes the name of his mother to make God feel obliged: 'Give your strength to your servant; save the child of your serving-maid' (v. 16). It's easy to start thinking this way. We all feel sometimes that God owes us one.

I don't think, however, that this is quite what the psalmist is doing. His sufferings are genuine: 'for to you do I cry all day long' (v. 3). His prayer therefore marshals every possible argument for believing that God will help: God's nature—'you, O Lord, are good and forgiving, abounding in steadfast love' (v. 5); God's uniqueness —'there is none like you' (v. 8); God's power—'you are great and do wondrous things' (v. 10); his own experience—'you have delivered my soul' (v. 13). All this may not be needed to persuade God; but it will certainly make the psalmist feel better!

Finally, he dares to ask for a sign, diplomatically pointing out that this is not for himself, but so that others will be convinced. God's attitude to those who ask for signs is ambivalent: he was patient with Gideon (Judges 6:39), but Jesus called those who asked for signs 'an evil and adulterous generation' (Matthew 12:39).

Yet God also invites us to 'taste and see' (Psalm 34:8); we are meant to experience grace, not just to know about it. Perhaps what the psalmist is really asking is, in the words of the song, 'Don't talk of love; show me.'

PRAYER

Show me, Lord!

48

CITY OF GOD

PSALM 87:1–3, 5–7

On the holy mount stands the city he founded; the Lord loves the gates of Zion more than all the dwellings of Jacob. Glorious things are spoken of you, O city of God… And of Zion it shall be said, 'This one and that one were born in it'; for the Most High himself will establish it. The Lord records, as he registers the peoples, 'This one was born there.' Singers and dancers alike say, 'All my springs are in you.'

'I belong to Glasgow, Glasgow belongs to me!' So sings the drunk in a well-worn comedy act. Many of us, entirely sober, feel a special affection for the place where we grew up. There are, however, other ways of belonging. I have neighbours who moved to our area 30 years ago, when they married, and have faithfully served God in the local church and community ever since. I'm sure they love their adopted suburb.

To belong to Jerusalem, for the Old Testament Jewish people, meant even more. It was not only their capital but the place where they met with God and each other, the source of spiritual refreshment. It is also destined to be the place where the whole world gathers to worship and serve the God of Israel: 'Many nations shall come and say: "Come, let us go up to the mountain of the Lord, to the house of the God of Jacob; that he may teach us his ways and that we may walk in his paths"' (Micah 4:2). As Christians, we await a new Jerusalem (Revelation 21:2), and meanwhile we are 'a city built on a hill' (Matthew 5:14).

I like the idea of God 'registering the peoples' and noting which ones belong to the holy city. It sounds like a generous divine immigration service, where everyone who applies can gain asylum. Our citizenship of God's kingdom is not dependent on how well we fulfil our calling. All it requires is that we are born into it—and not necessarily at an early age!

REFLECTION

'Jerusalem, Jerusalem, the city that kills the prophets and stones those who are sent to it! How often have I desired to gather your children together as a hen gathers her brood under her wings, and you were not willing!' (Luke 13:34).

—— 49 ——

TELLING IT STRAIGHT

PSALM 88:1–3, 6–9a

O Lord, God of my salvation, when, at night, I cry out in your presence, let my prayer come before you; incline your ear to my cry. For my soul is full of troubles, and my life draws near to Sheol... You have put me in the depths of the Pit, in the regions dark and deep. Your wrath lies heavy upon me, and you overwhelm me with all your waves. You have caused my companions to shun me; you have made me a thing of horror to them. I am shut in so that I cannot escape; my eye grows dim through sorrow.

For many years, living alone, I would wake up in the middle of night and my first thought would be, 'There is no God; I have been following an illusion.' I don't get those horrible feelings any more, but because of them I can understand the opening of this psalm: depression, fear and anxiety are always worst in the small hours. The writer describes the sensations powerfully: like being overwhelmed by a tidal wave, like being punished by God, like being the only person left on earth.

The knee-jerk reaction is to say something like, 'Come on, it can't be that bad—God will fix it.' Those who counsel the unhappy know that this only makes the feelings worse. The psalmist is brave enough to stay with the negative feelings, with no easy answers. He has no qualms about blaming God for his troubles. 'Why do you cast me off? Why do you hide your face from me?' (v. 14).

This may look like lack of faith; but it's the exact opposite. It takes a lot of faith to keep crying out to God when you can't see even a tiny speck of light at the end of the tunnel. Even if you're swearing at God, at least you're still talking. 'Every day I call on you, O Lord; I spread out my hands to you' (v. 9).

'Because this widow keeps bothering me,' says the judge in Jesus' parable, 'I will grant her justice... And will not God grant justice to his chosen ones who cry to him day and night?' (Luke 18:5, 7). Christians are sometimes nicknamed 'God-botherers'; that's just what we should be.

PRAYER

Save us from the time of trial! Deliver us from evil!

PERPLEXITY AND PRAISE

PSALM 89:1–4, 38–39, 49–52 (ABRIDGED)

I will sing of your steadfast love, O Lord, forever; with my mouth I will proclaim your faithfulness to all generations… You said, 'I have made a covenant with my chosen one, I have sworn to my servant David: "I will establish your descendants forever."' …

But now you have spurned and rejected him… You have renounced the covenant with your servant; you have defiled his crown in the dust… Lord, where is your steadfast love of old, which by your faithfulness you swore to David? Remember, O Lord, how your servant is taunted… Blessed be the Lord for ever. Amen and Amen.

At my church we sing an upbeat song, 'I have made a covenant with my chosen', based on this psalm. It's interesting, though, that the song makes no reference to the more negative parts of the psalm!

We started this series with questions about why the wicked don't suffer; we end with questions about why God's chosen people do. Again the writer thinks of every argument he can as to why God should rescue them: 'You promised' (v. 3); 'You created us' (vv. 9–13); 'You are just' (v. 14); 'You chose us' (vv. 19–37). He acknowledges that God's blessings are conditional on the people practising God's justice, but now God seems to have withdrawn the blessing, and the people don't even know what they've done wrong.

Most distressing is the impression that God has reneged on the promise to King David: 'I will establish his line for ever, and his throne as long as the heavens endure' (v. 29). How can this come true if David's people are utterly defeated and taken into exile?

I wonder whether the disciples, on the sabbath day after Jesus was crucified, read this psalm. It would certainly have given a voice to their desperate questions: they too had been given an 'anointed one', a successor to David, and yet now he was dead. What did it all mean?

Holy Saturday is, in a sense, where we are all living. We know about resurrection, but we don't always experience it. This psalm can give voice to our questions, too: where is the promised kingdom? But notice: the psalm begins and ends in praise. Amen and Amen.

PRAYER

Yours is the kingdom, the power and the glory.

✢

THE PRICKING OF MY THUMBS

As a child, I loved Tove Jansson's marvellous *Finn Family Moomintroll* children's stories. Imagine my joy when, on a visit to Finland, I had the opportunity to visit Moominworld—the most delightful and unDisney-like theme park I've ever been to! A character in my favourite Moomin book, the Muskrat, has a book on *The Uselessness of Everything*. When it is lost and restored by the Hobgoblin's magic, it has turned into *The Usefulness of Everything*. This *Woman Alive* column is on the usefulness of pain. Yes, really!

I hate to disagree with an expert, but... No, that's not true, I love to disagree and indulge in a moment of delicious 'righteous' anger— don't we all? Isn't that why we love to watch talk shows, and shout at the telly, 'What a load of old codswallop'?

But I digress (another thing I love to do). To return to the expert in question, I encountered him via an article of his in *Woman Alive*, which is why I hesitate (if not hate) to disagree with him. What he wrote was roughly as follows: he separated emotions into 'positive' feelings—joy, fulfilment, gratitude, peace, well-being—and what he defined as 'dark side' emotions—depression, emptiness, jealousy, anger, guilt.

Now I'm not about to praise my constant enemy of the last 25 years, depression. I can't say I actually enjoy feeling any of the others either—with the possible exception of anger, as hinted above! But I am very, very doubtful as to whether emotions can be so neatly separated into the good and the bad, the light and the dark.

Let me illustrate by an analogy. Take someone who suffers from leprosy (nowadays generally known as Hansen's disease). The disease destroys the nerve endings, leading to a loss of sensation in the skin. Sufferers gradually lose the ability to feel physical pain.

Hence they begin to injure themselves and, potentially, others. The patient doesn't feel it when he has a piece of grit in his eye. He blinks, and doesn't notice the damage being done. Eventually he may lose his sight. The mother with the disease touches a hot pan but fails to feel the resulting burn. She leaves the pan around, and her toddler touches it next... When you see pictures of sufferers with missing fingers or toes, it isn't because the condition makes limbs drop off; it's because it takes away our capacity to feel our own injuries.

Are you beginning to get the point? Physical pain is God's good gift to us, to let us know when we are damaging ourselves. And the pain that others express may let us know when we are damaging them. If this is so, is it not also true of emotional pain?

Let's return to that old enemy, depression. The Christian psychiatrist M. Scott Peck writes in his book *The Road Less Travelled* (Arrow, 1990, pp. 72–75) of the 'essential healthiness of depression'. By this he means that if you get depressed, your soul is alerting you to the fact that some emotion, some need, is not being heard. The healthy person reacts if something goes physically wrong inside them: they feel a pain, and if the cause isn't treated the pain may become acute or chronic. It's just the same with things that go emotionally wrong.

I suspect that the same applies to the other emotions denigrated by our expert friend. Feelings of emptiness may be telling you that something is empty about your life! Jealousy alerts you to any discontent with your own situation and can lead you to reassess your self-image or priorities. Anger is certainly healthy if there is something legitimate to be angry about, and if not, it exposes your inner weaknesses like nothing else does. Guilt may be a bad motivator, but if you've done something genuinely wrong and *don't* feel it, then people should start worrying about you!

I believe that God has given us all these emotions as the psychological equivalent of the sharp sensation you feel when, barefooted, you tread on a drawing pin left on the floor from your child's craft homework. Pain, said C.S. Lewis famously, is God's megaphone to rouse a deaf world (*The Problem of Pain*, Fount). Is that why many of us feel a slight unease about Christians who claim to live in unbroken joy, peace, and so on? Either they're lying, or perhaps they are developing a form of 'spiritual leprosy' many times more dangerous than the physical sort.

It may also be that 'negative' emotions are a built in 'evil detector' like that of Macbeth's witches: 'By the pricking of my thumbs, something wicked this way comes.' George Macdonald, in *The Princess and Curdie*, gave one of his characters the ability to take someone's hand and feel the paw of the beast they were becoming. I don't suppose it was a very pleasant gift to have, but enormously useful .

That's the point, really. None of these feelings is pleasant, but they are all essential to knowing what is going on inside ourselves and others. And they are the feelings that God chose to take on when he came as an infant at Christmas to share our joys *and our pains*. The only one I'm not sure he ever felt was true guilt—but then, perhaps, when he was made 'sin for us' on the cross (2 Corinthians 5:21), he felt that too. And that was the biggest gift of all.

JOEL: DISASTER AND PROMISE

Have you ever seen a locust invasion? Nor have I. But if you are reading this in the countryside, especially if you are a farmer, you will have a better chance of understanding Joel than if you are city-bred like me—and even more so if you are reading it in a developing country.

Here in the industrial (and temperate) West, we are shielded from the effects of many natural disasters. But for Joel's contemporaries, crop failure, for whatever reason, was an ever-present threat. No supermarkets, no exotic food imports for them. Joel's prophecies were given in the context of a plague of all-devouring locusts, which was followed by drought and then by destructive bush fires. The result was famine.

Most of us in Britain live far removed from the process of producing food, but it only takes a moment to realize that even factory workers, hospital staff, teachers or managers need to eat. Ultimately we are all dependent on the land—our own or someone else's.

On whom, then, does the land depend for its fertility? For Joel there was only one answer: God. If there was a disaster, it was only because God had allowed it. And why? Because the people of the land had not lived as God commanded.

We may not make such a simple equation between sin and disaster. (Are the people of Bangladesh or Sudan more sinful than us Westerners?) But we know—today perhaps more than ever—that there is a link between selfish human actions and environmental threats. Many 'natural disasters' are due to human short-termism, not what the insurance companies call 'acts of God'.

Joel probably wrote in the fifth century BC, in the southern nation of Judah, the area around Jerusalem (the old northern kingdom of Israel had long been destroyed). He may have been addressing discouraged returnees from the exile in Babylon, a poor nation with little infrastructure and little hope.

Yet his poetic prophecies move from immediate tragedy to a shining hope of the ultimate restoration of God's people and judgment of those who do evil. We may not suffer famine, but there are many other happenings in life that shake our faith. The hope that Joel holds out is relevant to all of us, at all times.

51

FIRST THE BAD NEWS

JOEL 1:1–4

The word of the Lord that came to Joel son of Pethuel: Hear this, O elders, give ear, all inhabitants of the land! Has such a thing happened in your days, or in the days of your ancestors? Tell your children of it, and let your children tell their children, and their children another generation.

What the cutting locust left, the swarming locust has eaten. What the swarming locust left, the hopping locust has eaten, and what the hopping locust left, the destroying locust has eaten.

As I write, Britain is recovering from a foot-and-mouth disease epidemic. Farming and the country's tourist industry were severely affected, but no one is starving. Most of us can always find sources of food and the money to pay for them. If your house floods, there is insurance; if your business goes under, there are welfare benefits or sometimes even compensation.

For ancient peoples, however, an invasion of locusts was a life-threatening event. They were compared to a cavalry army thundering in to destroy everything. Just as the Inuits of the Arctic have many words for snow, so Hebrew has nine words for the types and stages of growth of the locust (four are used in these verses). Language reflects what we live with on a daily basis.

This kind of disaster, Joel says, should never be forgotten. With famines, civil wars and massacres broadcast almost daily into our homes, we are apt to suffer from a modern disease: 'compassion fatigue'. But 'suffer' is not the right word; we switch off our sympathy in order *not* to suffer. It is the victims that continue suffering—and continue to tell the story.

Can we 'rich Christians' also continue telling it, for the sake of those who live daily with 'the wolf at the door'? No one will be interested in hearing our good news unless we have first heard and empathized with their bad news.

REFLECTION

'They asked only one thing, that we remember the poor' (Galatians 2:10). 'Has not God chosen the poor in the world to be... heirs of the kingdom?' (James 2:5). How will the poor be remembered in your church this week, as you worship one who 'for your sakes became poor' (2 Corinthians 8:9)?

52

ROBBED OF JOY

JOEL 1:11–13

Be dismayed, you farmers, wail, you vine-dressers, over the wheat and the barley; for the crops of the field are ruined. The vine withers, the fig tree droops. Pomegranate, palm, and apple—all the trees of the field are dried up; surely, joy withers away among the people.

Put on sackcloth and lament, you priests; wail, you ministers of the altar. Come, pass the night in sackcloth, you ministers of my God! Grain-offering and drink-offering are withheld from the house of your God.

My son wanted our garden shower on, the other hot day. Under the old 'water rates' system, I used water without thinking. Now that we're on a meter and pay for what we use, I hesitate a little. Perhaps it's good for me to think of clean water as precious. For millions in water-starved areas, drought is an annual reality. Imagine the varied, colourful piles of fresh produce in your local supermarket; then replace them in your mind with bare, cracked earth. That was Judah's plight after plague and drought.

It is hardly surprising that Joel encourages the farmers to express their grief. He has already addressed the wine drinkers (v. 5) who have lost their source of relaxation after a hard day. Now he turns to the priests who help the people to find joy in offering the best fruits of their labour. For the Hebrew mind, work, wine and worship were all part of the good rhythm of life given by God.

The deepest pain of plague and drought, then, is not just the hunger and thirst. It is that the people have lost the point of their work, the pleasure of social time and the joy of offering thanks to God. Their lives as well as their stomachs have become empty.

Often, after natural disaster, the churches or other places of worship are rebuilt first. People know instinctively that 'the things of the spirit' are at the heart of recreating their community.

When bad things happen to us, is our instinct to stay away from church, ashamed of not 'living in victory'— or to seek help there?

PRAYER

'The church is the only army that shoots its own wounded' (source unknown). May our churches be places where the wounded know that healing is available.

53

A CALL TO ACTION

JOEL 2:1–2a, 11

Blow the trumpet in Zion; sound the alarm on my holy mountain! Let all the inhabitants of the land tremble, for the day of the Lord is coming, it is near—a day of darkness and gloom, a day of clouds and thick darkness! ... The Lord utters his voice at the head of his army; how vast is his host! Numberless are those who obey his command. Truly the day of the Lord is great; terrible indeed—who can endure it?

Older readers will remember the ominous sound of air raid warnings, and perhaps still tremble when they hear that sound on an old film or documentary. For Israel, the dreaded sound was the trumpet blown to signal the approach of an enemy army, calling the women and children to shelter and the men to battle. Joel's thoughts have passed naturally from the cavalry charge of the unstoppable locusts to the sadly familiar scenario of human armies arriving to pillage and burn.

From there, he moves to the sounding of the 'last trumpet' announcing God's day of judgment. To the people of Israel, this was seen as the day when the enemy would 'get what's coming to them'. But Joel reminds them that judgment begins with God's own people. For them (us?) too, it will be 'a day of darkness'—unless they, like the avenging angel army, obey God's commands.

But the ram's horn trumpet could also herald a sacred fast, a day of repentance. Indeed, it is still used by Jews to begin the annual Day of Atonement. A warning is always just that: a chance to take action before the calamity falls.

When disasters happen, people have always asked 'whose fault?'

But Jesus, discussing 'those eighteen who were killed when the tower of Siloam fell on them', said, 'Do you think that they were worse offenders than all the others living in Jerusalem? No, I tell you; but unless you repent, you will all perish just as they did' (Luke 13:4–5). We cannot tell why; but we can all ask how we respond to life's uncertainties.

PRAYER

'Cry out to the Lord' is Joel's call to all the people (1:14). Cry out to God for one suffering group of people in the world today.

54

A TIME TO TEAR

JOEL 2:12–14

Yet even now, says the Lord, return to me with all your heart, with fasting, with weeping, and with mourning; rend your hearts and not your clothing. Return to the Lord, your God, for he is gracious and merciful, slow to anger, and abounding in steadfast love, and relents from punishing. Who knows whether he will not turn and relent, and leave a blessing behind him, a grain-offering and a drink-offering for the Lord, your God?

When our dog was run over, soon after my brother's death, my mother ran into the garden and began to tear leaves off the magnolia tree. Something deep within drove her to tear things in her grief. Orthodox Jews still tear their lapels to show mourning, as the Old Testament priests and people tore their robes to symbolize grief or repentance.

Joel calls for the outward sign to be matched by a wholehearted commitment to 'turn' to a new way of life. Although Joel portrays God 'turning' in response, this is not a change of mind on God's part, for God always has the same mind towards us: grace, mercy, steadfast love. It is more a change in how that love is expressed— not by judgment, which is no longer needed, but by gift.

Parents are used to small children handing back what they have just been given—a biscuit, perhaps—as 'a present for you, Mummy'. Adults expect to make or buy their own gifts, but in relation to God we are all like that little child. We can only give what God has given us. So the offerings here come from the harvest first given by God, who will restore fertility to the land.

In the act of repentance that prepares for this gift, the whole community is invited to take part: 'assemble the aged; gather the children, even infants at the breast. Let the bridegroom leave his room, and the bride her canopy' (2:16). What does this say to our tendency to make 'family' services upbeat, and reserve solemn occasions (for example, Ash Wednesday or Good Friday) for adults only?

REFLECTION

Think about the place of 'fasting, weeping and mourning' in your spiritual journey, alone and with others. Can you discuss this with a group?

55

GRAIN, GRAPE—AND SPIRIT

JOEL 2:18–19a, 28–29

Then the Lord became jealous for his land, and had pity on his people. In
response to his people the Lord said: I am sending you grain, wine, and oil,
and you will be satisfied… Then afterwards I will pour out my spirit on all
flesh; your sons and your daughters shall prophesy, your old men shall dream
dreams, and your young men shall see visions. Even on the male and female
slaves, in those days, I will pour out my spirit.

Even in the midst of scolding her child, a mother will turn to defend
that child from criticism by another. 'Do not make your heritage…
a byword among the nations' is the prayer that Joel recommends
(2:17) to the priests as they pray for deliverance. And in God's
response we find, as well as plentiful harvest, the promise, 'I will no
more make you a mockery among the nations' (v. 19b).

Why is God so 'jealous' for the reputation of the chosen people?
Does it matter what other nations, peoples with different values,
think of them? Yes, because the very thing they are chosen for is to
be 'a light to the nations' (Isaiah 49:6). If Israel loses its
distinctiveness, the surrounding peoples will have only darkness.

Under the new covenant, this role is taken by Jesus (see Luke
2:32), and then by his body, the Church. We are the light on a
lampstand, the city on a hill, the salt which must not lose its taste.
How can we live up to this calling? Only by the Holy Spirit poured
out on all—Joel's inspired vision, famously quoted by Peter at
Pentecost (Acts 2:17–21). In his picture of restoration, Joel moves
far beyond God's gift of grain and grapes (so sure is he of this that
he puts it in the past tense) to a gift inconceivable to Old Testament

people: the Spirit poured out even on the lowest of all, the female slave (v. 29). 'They shall all know me, from the least of them to the greatest' (Jeremiah 31:34).

REFLECTION

'All these won God's approval because of their faith; and yet they did not receive what was promised, because, with us in mind, God had made a better plan, that only with us should they reach perfection' (Hebrews 11:39–40, REB).

56

INTERNATIONAL JUSTICE

JOEL 2:30—3:2 (ABRIDGED)

I will show portents in the heavens and on the earth, blood and fire and columns of smoke. The sun shall be turned to darkness, and the moon to blood, before the great and terrible day of the Lord comes. Then everyone who calls on the name of the Lord shall be saved...

I will gather all the nations and bring them down to the valley of Jehoshaphat, and I will enter into judgment with them there, on account of my people and my heritage Israel, because they have scattered them among the nations.

'And we will all be called as witnesses, each and every one, To speak what was done,' says Paul Simon's stirring song 'Jerusalem'. As I write, former president Slobodan Milosevic of Serbia is on trial for war crimes at the International Court in the Hague. We strive for justice on earth, but Joel's 'end-times' vision promises a much greater tribunal. Will Ghengis Khan, Nero and Hitler at last get the full penalty for their crimes?

Jesus' teaching draws on these images of global disaster (for example, Mark 13:24–25). It's notable, too, that Peter's sermon in Acts 2 includes this terrifying part of Joel's prophecy. But the key is the verse where Peter stops: 'everyone who calls on the name of the Lord will be saved' (Acts 2:21). That offer goes beyond ancient Israel: 'People will come from east and west, from north and south, and will eat in the kingdom of God' (Luke 13:29).

The hope for restoration must always include a hope for retribution. Joel's list of crimes against Israel has a horrible contemporary ring: 'They have divided my land... and traded boys for prostitutes,

148

and sold girls for wine…' (3:3). The final reckoning includes not only 'what was done' to the Jews, but also to the Armenians, the Tutsis, the East Timorese, the Palestinians—all the persecuted peoples of the world. The day is coming… rejoice.

PRAYER

'I saw under the altar the souls of those who had been slaughtered for the word of God and for the testimony they had given; they cried out with a loud voice, "Sovereign Lord… how long will it be before you judge and avenge our blood?"' (Revelation 6:9–10). Make 'How long?' your own prayer.

57

VENGEANCE IS GOD'S

JOEL 3:9–13, 19–21 (ABRIDGED)

Proclaim this among the nations: Prepare war, stir up the warriors... Bring down your warriors, O Lord... Put in the sickle, for the harvest is ripe. Go in, tread, for the wine press is full. The vats overflow, for their wickedness is great...

Egypt shall become a desolation and Edom a desolate wilderness, because of the violence done to the people of Judah, in whose land they have shed innocent blood... I will avenge their blood, and I will not clear the guilty, for the Lord dwells in Zion.

Battle and destruction seem a negative place to end our notes, but it's where Joel ends his prophecies. Is it a threat or a promise? For Judah's enemies, certainly a threat: their land will become as barren as Judah's is now. But for Judah, it's a promise: the atrocities committed against them will be avenged.

In preparation for this great reversal, Joel advises the pagan nations to 'beat your ploughshares into swords, and your pruning-hooks into spears' (v. 10). It's the opposite of what Isaiah promises (Isaiah 2:4), so what has happened to the vision of peace, so precious to my own, pacifist, church?

The defeat of evil is a difficult issue. Who will do the defeating? In Britain, two young men have just finished their prison sentences for the murder of a two-year-old boy, committed when they were both aged ten. There was a furore at their release. Their identities have been changed, for fear of revenge.

Are we justified in waging war against wrongdoers? True, Jesus said, 'I have not come to bring peace, but a sword' (Matthew

10:34). Yet he also said, 'All who take the sword will perish by the sword'(Matthew 26:52). And his followers called him the Prince of Peace.

Joel is not necessarily predicting literal war any more than a literal harvest. These are pictures of the seriousness of the verdict on evil. His advice to the pagan warriors is ironic; what chance have they against God? Nor can God's people finally defeat evil by the further evil of war. It is God alone who says, 'I will sit to judge' (v. 12).

PRAYER

'The Son of God was revealed for this purpose, to destroy the works of the devil' (1 John 3:8). Praise God for Jesus.

✛

WHERE DOES IT HURT?

So where do we go when our whole life seems to be falling apart? Whom can we tell, and who will speak for us? Many of us would much sooner go to a psychotherapist than to their church leaders or Christian friends (I have nothing against psychotherapists, by the way—I go to one myself). Often our Christian experience has taught us that grief or depression, or ill health that does not go away with one prayer, are not welcome in a church where life is supposed to be easy and full of joy as soon as we've decided to follow Jesus. Hence this column, which explores how we might acknowledge pain within worship.

It was not quite the response I had expected to my routine question, 'How are you?' Without any hesitation, Frederica replied, 'All right, but I've got this nasty graze on my knee.' She then proceeded to lift her voluminous skirts, show me the scab and then peel it off in a long strip, as uninhibited as a child.

Frederica is a lady of mature years and considerable intellect, who lectures on Greek philosophy and has competed in the semi-final of a high-powered radio quiz show. She lives alone, which is perhaps why she has acquired some eccentric habits with regard to scabs.

But I was rather touched by her lack of reserve. For some reason, I couldn't help wondering how her knee-exposing act might have gone down in the average church. What if she'd done it in the middle of prayers, or during tea and 'fellowship' afterwards? Would it have put people off their Nice biscuits? Or off their 'nice' behaviour?

Some of us are very 'decently and in order' people—especially those who say, in the words of a recent letter I received, 'We're all Church of England, I hope' (no, we're not). Even in the places where you can swing from chandeliers, or at least wave your hands a bit, they might balk at public scab-picking.

But it's really the symbolism of the act that interests me. Some years ago, in a poem about exposing my feelings, I wrote the lines 'like a child letting the doctor/see where it hurts'. Those lines came back as I watched Frederica reveal the new skin on her knee. Can we, as Christians, reveal our wounds to each other in the same un-selfconscious way—or at all?

I read yesterday that prayers of complaint are the most common form of public prayer in the Bible (not a lot of people know that...). The Psalms, which contain some seriously whingeing 'official complaints to the management', are an obvious case. And this is hardly surprising, given the history of the Jewish people: we've had quite a lot to whinge about.

Drop in to the typical church today, and you will be hard pushed to find a single lament or even slight expression of doubt. Questioning God's ways in church? It's just not done. We don't even make audacious requests without buttering God up with a little fulsome praise first, just to get on the right side.

You may protest that we are under the new covenant now, where praise always takes precedence, and we have more to give praise for than the ancient Israelites did. But that's not the point. Praise formed a big part of their worship too, and they often prefaced their desires with a reminder to God (in case he'd forgotten) of all the good things he had done for them in the past.

The real difference between their worship and ours, however, is that in our recipe complaint does not figure at all, whereas in theirs it was a key ingredient. Could that be why our prayers sometimes seem rather insipid—a bit like guacamole with the chilli sauce inadvertently left out? Could it be, I dare to suggest, why we sometimes find it hard to perceive the answers?

After all, life, in my 50-plus years of experience, has not got significantly easier than it was for the writers of Psalms, Lamentations or Habakkuk ('Oh Lord, how long?'). Sure, in Christ we have a new understanding of God and a very different way of access to God. But if we do not use that access by being honest to God about the things that bug, frighten or overwhelm us, we are hardly likely to hear God's honest answer.

Personally I think that we need to do this, not just when no one is listening, but in the gathered people of God. What sense does it make to proclaim that we're one body, if the members aren't communicating freely with each other, let alone with the head? Shouldn't church be a place to expose our not-quite-healed-yet wounds to each other, as well as the new skin we're quite proud of?

In Mennonite churches there is a common practice of the 'sharing time', when anyone can announce things for which they need intercession or are thankful. It can descend to the mundane ('Our rabbit died'); but it can also be a powerhouse of community-building and even of mission. I heard recently of a Mennonite librarian who found himself invited to a meeting of the Michigan militia, one of the groups stockpiling arms for an expected confrontation with the US government. As a pacifist Daniel facing a gun-toting den of lions, he was terrified; and he told his church so. What a challenge to prayer and kingdom living!

My church likewise sometimes has a 'sharing time', and I think we need more. I'd like a space where I can safely say, 'Help, I lost my cool and threw a cup of water in my son's face the other day and I need your and God's forgiveness and support.' Wouldn't that make for a more 'real' church?

Whenever I sing that lovely modern hymn by Graham Kendrick, 'The Servant King', and get to 'Come see his hands and feet, the scars that speak of sacrifice', I always remember the words of St Teresa of Avila, 'God has no hands and feet now but ours to do his will on earth'. I think that these hands and feet have scars, too, which may speak of God's love in a lesser, but still powerful way. The risen Lord shows us his scars, and we worship; shouldn't we be free to show ours to him and each other, and worship?

SIGNS OF THE TIMES

Nearly 20 years ago, a small collection of my *Woman Alive* columns was published. Before sales could pick up (perhaps they never would have done?), all the unsold copies were destroyed in a warehouse fire. Please don't make any remarks about the former Bishop of Durham, lightning striking York Minster, and God's judgment on heresy…

Anyway, riffling through this ancient collection the other day, I encountered one that began like this:

It was the Christian paper that finally did it. 'I don't know if he's a Christian,' my friend confided, 'but I wrote to him on Christian paper.' 'Christian paper?' I wondered to myself. 'What on earth is that?' It turned out, as I had guessed, to be notepaper with a Bible verse on every sheet.

That was when I decided. And now I call several thousand readers to witness: I resolve that never, but never again will I use the word 'Christian' as an adjective to describe anything but people.

Well, I've probably broken that resolution a few times since then, speaking of such things as 'Christian thinking' (a useful shorthand for 'what most Christians believe'). I still think it was a good one, though.

The trouble with 'Christian' as an adjective for such things as notepaper is that it is yet another brick in our construction of a 'safe' Christian enclave in which nothing will enter that we might have to think about or evaluate, that might disturb or tempt us. In this process, I believe, we also reconstruct Jesus. We construct a Jesus who is very concerned about his people's 'purity', who will have nothing to do with 'sinners', who is deeply upset when we fall even a little from 100 per cent obedience, who is more concerned that we believe the right things than that we live as he lived—a Jesus, in fact, who is the exact opposite of the one who actually lived and who appears in the Gospels!

The Jesus I see in the Gospels is like this: he freely breaks the rules for the benefit of the needy; he loves best those who live in a constant struggle to survive; he actively dislikes those who strive for religious purity; he cares more about inner attitudes than outer respectability; he likes to party, and he constantly gets into trouble with the powers that be. That's the Jesus I first fell in love with over 35 years ago, and in whose name I took the very risky step of baptism. I knew it was not the entrance token to a life of niceness, but the membership card to a life of change, risk and loss.

I have written frequently about the need to read the rest of the Bible in the light of Jesus. The Gospel readings in the following section are a small attempt to introduce people to Jesus as I see him—a man who, I suspect, would be much more likely to ask whether the notepaper was fairly and sustainably traded than whether it had a Bible text on it.

One of his most striking characteristics is a great ability to link his message to the events and everyday life of his own time. He talked about farming, bread-baking, lost possessions, tenants and landlords, celebration dinners, natural and human-made disasters, house-building, getting into debt, and having a financial windfall. And he made all these things into signs of the kingdom that is coming but, in him, is also already here.

Following Jesus isn't about putting a religious stamp on everything you do, consume and create. It's about living the kind of generous, compassionate, just and God-filled life that he lived, in this world that we all have to live in.

Can we, like him, find 'signs of the times' in our world (which is, of course, really God's world)?

ADVENT: THE COMING OF GOD

....

'Jesus is coming; look busy!' reads a popular T-shirt slogan. The implication is that although he may have been 'meek and mild' (oh yeah?) the first time, the second time around we're really going to be in trouble if we don't get our act together.

Advent, for which the following notes were written, is a time when we remember Jesus' coming to us as a baby and also look forward to his coming again to set the whole world to rights. But what sort of Jesus do we expect to come?

The T-shirt slogan is a caricature, of course, and I'm sure it wasn't a Christian who wrote it. But caricature succeeds best when it has just a grain of truth in it. It seems to me that Christians sometimes preach and believe that the Jesus who always showed compassion to the weak when he was a first-century Jew will, when he returns, mysteriously have turned into a person full of wrath, ready to send us to eternal torment for the slightest doubt on any doctrinal issue.

I'm always comforted by the words spoken by the angel at Jesus' ascension, in Acts 1:11, which in some translations (including the NIV) reads, '*This same Jesus*, who has been taken from you into heaven, will come back in the same way you have seen him go.' It's not a different Jesus, less compassionate, less merciful, who is going to return to judge the world. Indeed, he himself says, in John 12:47, 'I do not judge anyone who hears my words and does not keep them, for I came not to judge the world, but to save the world.'

So as we reflect in these notes on the many ways in which God comes to us, you may notice that 'God comes... in condemnation' is missing. That's deliberate!

Yes, there will come a time when God judges the lives of all who have lived. Remember, though, that God is infinitely more just than we are, so we should beware of portraying God as less so. And for those who have chosen to follow Jesus in their lives (and maybe even those who walked his way without knowing it: Romans 2:14–15), there is a place in the kingdom.

It helps, of course, if you have begun to practise living in the kingdom this side of death. And it is Jesus' first coming at Christmas that begins to open that kingdom to us.

58

GOD COMES... IN CREATION

GENESIS 1:26–28a, 31a

Then God said, 'Let us make humankind in our own image, according to our likeness; and let them have dominion over the fish of the sea, and over the birds of the air, and over the cattle, and over all the wild animals of the earth, and over every creeping thing that creeps upon the earth.' So God created humankind in his image, in the image of God he created them; male and female he created them. God blessed them, and God said to them, 'Be fruitful and multiply, and fill the earth and subdue it... God saw everything that he had made, and indeed, it was very good.

It was the low time of year—frost on the ground, fog in the air, everything in the garden looking dead and dismal. One morning, a rare day of sunshine, I pointed out the blue sky to my then two-year-old son and he said, 'Where's the other sky gone?' Grey skies had come to seem normal to him.

Perhaps your December world can look equally grim. The duties of Christmas, the cards still unwritten and presents unwrapped, the prospect of time with demanding relatives; in the midst of this, the reality of 'God with us' disappears like the garden under the fog.

It seems good, then, to start our Christmas build-up where the traditional 'Festival of Nine Lessons' starts: with the creation of the world. In a sense, this is where God first comes to us; as John Swanson put it, before the re-demption of the world comes the 'demption' (in Robert Llewelyn, ed., *Julian: Woman of our Day*, DLT, 1985). God claims us as his own first of all in our creation. God speaks, and makes a world; God speaks, and makes us to reflect and relate to him; God speaks to us and gives us the task of preserving and developing creation. And it is all very good. The only reason we celebrate Christmas is that 'God so loved the world' (John 3:16).

PRAYER

'By an act of understanding… be present now with all the creatures among which you live, and hear them in their beings and operations praising God in an heavenly manner… Can you take too much joy in your Father's works? He is himself in everything' (Thomas Traherne, 1637–74).

59

GOD COMES... IN OUR FAILURES

GENESIS 3:6–9

So when the woman saw that the tree was good for food, and that it was a delight to the eyes, and that the tree was to be desired to make one wise, she took of its fruit and ate; and she also gave some to her husband, who was with her, and he ate. Then the eyes of both were opened, and they knew that they were naked; and they sewed fig leaves together and made loincloths for themselves.

They heard the sound of the Lord God walking in the garden at the time of the evening breeze, and the man and his wife hid themselves from the presence of the Lord God among the trees of the garden. But the Lord God called to the man and said, 'Where are you?'

My mother still talks about the Christmas at least 40 years ago when the goose tasted of fish, and the one when the roast potatoes were hard in the middle, not to mention the two recent years when she cooked the turkey upside down. Christmas is a time when we set ourselves up for failure, expecting so much. Suicides and family break-ups peak at Christmas, as a time that is meant to be joyful becomes a time of stress, conflict or loneliness.

The Advent readings continue with the account of humankind's first and greatest failure. Don't blame Eve, or Adam; this is the story of all of us. 'I don't accomplish the good I set out to do, and the evil I don't really want to do I find I am always doing' (Romans 7:19, J.B. Phillips).

We sometimes talk as though our sin has made God turn away from us. But in this primal story of sin, God does not reject his disobedient children. It is they who hide from him (in the trees, the place of disobedience, as though wilfully clinging to their own failure). God, on the other hand, comes closer than ever: 'walking in the garden', as 'God with us' later walked in a garden after we had wounded him to the heart once more in the crucifixion. 'O happy fault', the Catholic service for Holy Saturday says, 'which has deserved to have such and so mighty a Redeemer.'

REFLECTION

In our disappointments and failings, can we hear God calling, 'Where are you?' What will we answer?

60

GOD COMES... IN CHANGE

GENESIS 18:1–2, 9–14

The Lord appeared to Abraham by the oaks of Mamre, as he sat at the entrance of his tent in the heat of the day. He looked up and saw three men standing near him. When he saw them, he ran from the tent entrance to meet them, and bowed down to the ground...

They said to him, 'Where is your wife Sarah?' And he said, 'There, in the tent.' Then one said, 'I will surely return to you in due season, and your wife Sarah shall have a son.' And Sarah was listening at the tent entrance behind him. Now Abraham and Sarah were old, advanced in age; it had ceased to be with Sarah after the manner of women. So Sarah laughed to herself, saying, 'After I have grown old, and my husband is old, shall I have pleasure?' The Lord said to Abraham, 'Why did Sarah laugh, and say, "Shall I indeed bear a child, now that I am old?" Is anything too wonderful for the Lord?'

'Yes, we did have a good Christmas overall,' replied my friend to my query. 'But every year our Christmas is exactly the same, and this year it was all different.' Most of us don't much like change. My father-in-law is known to his wife as 'Status Quo'; he likes to remain doing whatever he's doing, and, in my experience, his son and grandson take after him. (At least I can be sure my husband will stay married to me!)

Sarah had experienced 'the change of life' and wasn't prepared for any more change. As an 'elderly primigravida' myself, I know how she felt. Nothing changes your life as much as a baby. But this baby represented more than broken nights: Isaac would begin the out-working of God's promise to call a people as his own, a people through whom he would offer the world wholeness. And the baby we remember at Christmas, this time born to a mother too young, brings in the completion of that promise: 'the Light that will shine upon the nations, and... the glory of your people Israel' (Luke 2:32, LB).

God coming to Abraham in three men who appear and disappear mysteriously in the desert; God coming to us in an apparently 'illegitimate' baby born among the household animals. Both are hard to believe rationally, yet the story of a special birth bringing new life for the world still rings true and draws our wonder.

REFLECTION

'The hopes and fears of all the years are met in thee tonight' (O Little Town of Bethlehem)

GOD COMES... IN NEW LIFE

MATTHEW 1:18–23

Now the birth of Jesus the Messiah took place in this way. When his mother Mary had been engaged to Joseph, but before they lived together, she was found to be with child from the Holy Spirit. Her husband Joseph, being a righteous man and unwilling to expose her to public disgrace, planned to dismiss her quietly. But just when he had resolved to do this, an angel of the Lord appeared to him in a dream and said, 'Joseph, son of David, do not be afraid to take Mary as your wife, for the child conceived in her is from the Holy Spirit. She will bear a son, and you are to name him Jesus, for he will save his people from their sins.' All this took place to fulfil what had been spoken by the Lord through the prophet: 'Look, the virgin shall conceive and bear a son, and they shall name him Emmanuel', which means, 'God is with us.'

Isaiah's prophecy, in the original Hebrew, simply says that 'a young woman' will conceive a son (Isaiah 7:14): nothing unusual about that. It was the translators of the text into Greek, centuries before Jesus, who introduced the idea of a virgin conceiving, but maybe they were prophets too...

There's nothing unusual about being called Jesus, either. It's just the Greek version of Joshua, a name still popular in many a toddler group.

These were ordinary events, nothing to draw any attention—and maybe dozens of babies were born among cattle and laid in mangers around Israel at that time of mass displacement. It takes the eye of faith to see something extraordinary; the dreaming spirit of Joseph, named after another biblical dreamer, to see the Holy Spirit in what seemed at first a betrayal.

Because we know what happened afterwards, we see that this baby is in a unique way 'Emmanuel'. But in another sense, every birth is God coming to us with a new chance, for every new person is a mirror of God, a potential partner in God's remaking of the world. Some of us have the blessing and responsibility of nurturing that new life. All of us can seek the renewed life that God offers us all and share it with others. And what better time to do it than at Christmas?

PRAYER

Pray for anyone you know with a new baby, that in this new life they may meet the Creator God.

62

GOD COMES... IN THE NEEDY

MATTHEW 25:34–40 (ABRIDGED)

'Then the king will say to those at his right hand, "Come, you that are blessed by my Father, inherit the kingdom prepared for you from the foundation of the world; for I was hungry and you gave me food, I was thirsty and you gave me something to drink, I was a stranger and you welcomed me, I was naked and you gave me clothing, I was sick and you took care of me, I was in prison and you visited me." Then the righteous will answer him, "Lord, when was it that we saw you hungry and gave you food, or thirsty and gave you something to drink... a stranger and welcomed you, or naked and gave you clothing... sick or in prison and visited you?" And the king will answer them, "Truly I tell you, just as you did it to one of the least of these who are members of my family, you did it to me."'

'Good King Wenceslas looked out on the feast of Stephen...' (which is our Boxing Day). We know the rest: he saw a poor man gathering wood, and went out in the snow with his page to fetch the man and give him a feast. As the page trod in his master's footsteps, the ground was hot where the king had walked.

A woman I know was Christmas shopping on a freezing day when she saw three homeless men huddled in a doorway. She knew one from the local soup kitchen, and she greeted him. Then James' words came into her mind: 'If a brother or sister is naked and lacks daily food, and one of you says to them, "Go in peace; keep warm and eat your fill", and yet you do not supply their bodily needs, what is the good of that?' (James 2:15–16). Yards away was a stall selling warm hats and scarves. My friend bought the men a hat or scarf each, and that gift gave her more pleasure than any other.

God came to us at Christmas in a homeless family. In Jesus' parable he comes to us again in everyone in need. It may not be easy to see him in the heap of blankets on the street or the hand begging for change. But if we miss him, it is our own loss.

REFLECTION

'Ye who now will bless the poor shall yourselves find blessing' (Good King Wenceslas).

63

GOD COMES... IN TRANSFORMATION

REVELATION 21:1–5

Then I saw a new heaven and a new earth; for the first heaven and the first earth had passed away, and the sea was no more. And I saw the holy city, the new Jerusalem, coming down out of heaven from God, prepared as a bride adorned for her husband. And I heard a loud voice from the throne saying, 'See, the home of God is among mortals. He will dwell with them; they will be his peoples, and God himself will be with them; he will wipe every tear from their eyes. Death will be no more; mourning and crying and pain will be no more, for the first things have passed away.' And the one who was seated on the throne said, 'See, I am making all things new.'

In our reading from Genesis 3, God 'walked in the garden' when humankind had failed. Here, God 'dwells with mortals', not because of our success but because of the transformation of all things made possible by Jesus' coming, which will be complete when he comes again.

Having grown up far from the coast, I've always been rather disappointed that there is no sea in this vision of the new heaven and earth. But for the Middle Eastern folk who first read John's words, the sea represented all the forces of destruction in nature. The new world would be a place of safety, where sailors no longer went out to be drowned. Indeed, death would no longer take any of our loved ones.

Each Christmas Eve I remember my friend Kathy, who died of cancer on that day, leaving a daughter aged under two. Others I know remember spouses or family lost at Christmas. For everyone who is bereaved, the first Christmas with a place missing at the table is especially hard. I read this passage to my mother when my brother died just after Christmas over 30 years ago, for here God promises not only to stay with us, but to wipe away every tear.

REFLECTION

'In [Christ] all things in heaven and on earth were created... in him all things hold together... in him all the fullness of God was pleased to dwell, and through him God was pleased to reconcile to himself all things, whether on earth or in heaven, by making peace through the blood of his cross' (Colossians 1:16–20, abridged).

LUKE 13—17:
INCLUSIVE INVITATION

Have you ever heard a sermon that talks about 'the exclusive claims of Christ'? I must have heard a dozen. They're usually based on verses such as John 14:6: 'I am the way, and the truth, and the life. No one comes to the Father except through me.'

There's nothing wrong with trying to demonstrate that Jesus is different from other religious figures in history, but I always worry a little when I hear that phrase about 'exclusive claims'. To me, it seems only a small step from this phrase to building an exclusive church, one that only welcomes those who believe the same things as that particular Christian group.

I don't want to deny that in the Gospels Jesus says 'exclusive' things about himself—statements of a truth that necessarily excludes other 'truths'. At the same time I want to balance that with what I call the 'inclusive invitation' of Christ.

These chapters from the middle of Luke's Gospel are all about the kingdom of God as a great party to which everyone is invited without conditions; about God's search for everything and everyone who has been lost in any way; about cancellation of debts, welcome to sinners, freedom from illness and hunger. They are also about Jesus' call to a way of life that will cost us everything: a way that the rich may be unwilling to take and that those who prefer safety may turn away from.

Promise and challenge are the two poles of Jesus' ministry here: the promise of the inclusive invitation, and the challenge of the exclusive claims. We need to hold the tension between them and not overbalance into selecting only one or the other, as we read and as we teach.

64

CHALLENGED

LUKE 13:10–15 (ABRIDGED)

Now he was teaching in one of the synagogues on the sabbath. And just then there appeared a woman with a spirit that had crippled her for eighteen years. She was bent over and was quite unable to stand up straight. When Jesus saw her, he called her over and said, 'Woman, you are set free from your ailment.' When he laid his hands on her, immediately she stood up straight and began praising God. But the leader of the synagogue... kept saying to the crowd, 'There are six days on which work ought to be done; come on those days and be cured, and not on the sabbath day.' But the Lord answered him and said, 'You hypocrites! Does not each of you on the sabbath untie his ox or his donkey from the manger, and lead it away to give it water?'

I sometimes lead a workshop on this story, using a poem of mine called 'Upright'. The poem calls the woman 'half a person' and observes how people talk, literally, over her head. One workshop participant was reminded of the servants she'd seen in South America, hunched from carrying others' burdens; another thought of his mother, confined to a wheelchair by arthritis. There are many ways we can be 'bent double'—disability, mental illness, poverty—whether or not we blame it on 'a spirit'.

The most exciting thing here is the way Jesus takes the initiative. The woman has not asked for healing. Jesus himself calls her, breaking through her fear and shyness. Then, when questioned, he gives her an unheard-of title: 'daughter of Abraham' (v. 16). She is a full human being, heir to all God's promises.

The challenge to the Pharisees is to see this outsider as more valuable than their livestock. If they would 'bend' the sabbath for animals, how much more should they do so for a human being!

To stand upright and look people in the eye is to value yourself as God values you. It is also quite scary after years of being bowed down. The challenge to the woman—and to us—is to know our value in God's eyes. Then we can truly value and love others as ourselves.

REFLECTION

'You are precious in my sight… and I love you' (Isaiah 43:4).

65

TICKET TO HEAVEN?

LUKE 13:23–27

Someone asked [Jesus], 'Lord, will only a few be saved?' He said to them, 'Strive to enter through the narrow door; for many, I tell you, will try to enter and will not be able. When once the owner of the house has got up and shut the door, and you begin to stand outside and to knock at the door, saying, "Lord, open to us", then in reply he will say to you, "I do not know where you come from." Then you will begin to say, "We ate and drank with you, and you taught in our streets." But he will say, "I do not know where you come from; go away from me, all you evildoers!"'

'Book early to avoid disappointment' say the adverts for theatre shows. Many have thought of God's kingdom similarly: there are only so many places, so who will get in?

But Jesus said, 'In my Father's house there are many dwelling-places' (John 14:2). He is not interested in excluding people from the kingdom, but in inviting them. So why does he warn here about the door being shut?

First, the issue is not the space available, but the right time to come. If you arrive after the play has started, you won't get in, however many seats are free. 'Today if you hear his voice, do not harden your hearts' (Hebrews 4:7). God's mercy is unlimited, but we may not always be capable of receiving it. We can only get through the narrow door if we let him free us of baggage.

Second, salvation is bigger than just 'securing our booking'. A ticket is no use if you don't know the route to the theatre! Knowing about Jesus, even talking to him, means nothing if we are 'evildoers'. 'You are my friends if you do what I command you' (John 15:14).

The good we do is the sign that we know him. Many who claim to be 'in' with him may find themselves outside; and others who hardly dared to hope will be welcomed in, 'and will eat in the kingdom of God' (Luke 13:29).

REFLECTION

'Show me your faith without deeds, and I will show you my faith by what I do' (James 2:18, NIV).

66

FOX AND HEN

LUKE 13:31–34

At that very hour some Pharisees came and said to him, 'Get away from here, for Herod wants to kill you.' He said to them, 'Go and tell that fox for me, "Listen, I am casting out demons and performing cures today and tomorrow, and on the third day I finish my work. Yet today, tomorrow and the next day I must be on my way, because it is impossible for a prophet to be killed away from Jerusalem." Jerusalem, Jerusalem, the city that kills the prophets and stones those who are sent to it! How often have I desired to gather your children together as a hen gathers her brood under her wings, and you were not willing!'

Visiting friends in the countryside, I noticed on the lawn a pathetic pile of feathers. It was all that the local fox had left of one of my friends' hens.

If Herod is a fox and Jesus a mother hen, we might guess which is likely to win the battle. The warning, from some sympathetic Pharisees, is apparently timely, but Jesus turns the tables. The 'three days' signify the short time he still has left. He will let nothing stop him from using this time to the full—neither sabbath rules, nor speculative questions, nor danger. 'My Father is still working, and I also am working' (John 5:17).

Jesus is not a strutting, aggressive rooster, facing down the fox. The mother hen is both vulnerable and protective. There is a great sadness about her desire to shelter her chicks, when all they seem to want to do is run into the clutches of the fox. Jerusalem, built as the city of peace, has rarely 'recognized the things that make for peace' (Luke 19:42).

No wonder Jesus weeps as he makes his final journey into the fated city. Too often, the very people God chooses are the ones who fail to hear his voice. There is both a warning and an invitation here: the wings of the mother hen are still ready to gather us, if we are willing.

PRAYER

Imagine yourself safe under God's wings (read Psalm 91:1–6 for a fuller picture). From this protected position, ask if there is a message you need to hear.

67

SEATING PLANS

LUKE 14:1, 7–11 (ABRIDGED)

On one occasion when Jesus was going to the house of a leader of the Pharisees to eat a meal on the sabbath, they were watching him closely…

When he noticed how the guests chose the places of honour, he told them a parable. 'When you are invited by someone to a wedding banquet, do not sit down at the place of honour, in case someone more distinguished than you has been invited by your host; and the host who invited both of you may come and say to you, "Give this person your place." … But when you are invited, go and sit down at the lowest place, so that when your host comes, he may say to you, "Friend, move up higher." … For all who exalt themselves will be humbled, and those who humble themselves will be exalted.'

Have you ever had to make seating plans for a wedding? It's agonizing: dare we sit deaf Aunt Charlotte next to rude Uncle Dennis, and do we want to invite them anyway?

It's much simpler, as in Jesus' day, to let the guests sort themselves out according to their own view of their importance. Or is it? On the surface, Jesus' advice is just a way of avoiding embarrassment for those with an inflated idea of their status. But this is about more than etiquette, and the occasion is more than the girl next door's wedding. Throughout the Gospels, parables about feasts look forward to God's coming kingdom, the greatest party of all.

In the kingdom, the normal values about who's at the top and bottom of society are totally reversed. 'He has brought down the powerful from their thrones, and lifted up the lowly,' said Mary prophetically (Luke 1:52). And Jesus, speaking to priests and elders, echoes, 'The tax collectors and the prostitutes are going into the kingdom of God ahead of you' (Matthew 21:31). The most unlikely people (worse than Uncle Dennis…) are getting invitations.

Who gets the 'places of honour' in your church, or your local community? 'The kings of the Gentiles lord it over them… But not so with you' (Luke 22:25–26).

REFLECTION

'Has not God chosen the poor in the world to be rich in faith and to be heirs of the kingdom? (James 2:5).

— 68 —

GUEST LISTS

LUKE 14:16–23 (ABRIDGED)

Then Jesus said… 'Someone gave a great dinner and invited many. At the time for the dinner he sent his slave to say to those who had been invited, "Come; for everything is ready now." But they all alike began to make excuses… Then the owner of the house became angry and said to his slave, "Go out at once into the streets and lanes of the town and bring in the poor, the crippled, the blind, and the lame." And the slave said, "Sir, what you ordered has been done, and there is still room." Then the master said to the slave, "Go out into the roads and lanes, and compel people to come in, so that my house may be filled."'

At a leading Pharisee's house, these words would have been dynamite. No educated Jew could miss the references. The 'great dinner' was obviously the kingdom of God, when all the world would live in peace and justice. 'Those who had been invited' could only be the Jewish people themselves, who had been privileged with the gift of the law and prophets.

The poor and disabled, however, were those who had been excluded from the chosen people as 'not good enough'. No one with a disability could worship in the temple; and the poor had no leisure for religion, or money for lavish sacrifices.

But the kingdom that Jesus (the 'owner's slave') announces is radically different. The poor, blind and lame are the very people for whom he has come, as Luke showed us early on: 'He has anointed me to bring good news to the poor… release to the captives… sight to the blind' (Luke 4:18). Those who were invited first have already gone their own way; and it is noticeable that their excuses were all

180
180

to do with 'property' of one kind or another (including wives...)

Which group of guests do we identify with: the official guest list, or the street and lane dwellers? And which do we invite to 'eat bread in the kingdom of God'? If 'the righteous'—the well-off, respectable, moral—are no longer responding, perhaps we should be going out to meet some 'sinners' (see Luke 5:31).

PRAYER

Lord, show me and my church who is ready to feast with God.

——— 69 ———

COST-BENEFIT ANALYSIS

LUKE 14:25–31 (ABRIDGED)

Now large crowds were travelling with him; and he turned and said to them, 'Whoever comes to me and does not hate father and mother, wife and children, brothers and sisters, yes, and even life itself, cannot be my disciple. Whoever does not carry the cross and follow me cannot be my disciple. For which of you, intending to build a tower, does not first sit down and estimate the cost, to see whether he has enough to complete it? ... Or what king, going out to wage war against another king, will not sit down first and consider whether he is able with ten thousand to oppose the one who comes against him with twenty thousand?'

In my Mennonite church tradition, we have a book called *Martyrs Mirror* (Thieleman J. Van Braght, Herald Press, 2003), an account of early followers of that tradition who were tortured and killed (mostly by other Christians). They included mothers who left young families and were burnt alive for the freedom to worship as they believed right—and still sang praises as they died.

When Jesus spoke, the shadow of the cross for dissidents loomed as large as the stake did for 16th-century Anabaptists. How many of the 'large crowds' hovered uncertainly at the edge or turned away at this point?

Recently, as a young woman joined our church, I pondered how her Christian faith might reduce her chances of finding a marriage partner in the small 'Christian world'. The sacrifice she is making is not life-threatening, but it highlights the fact that there is still a cost to discipleship. In some places, the risk may, even today, be persecution or death.

None of us likes 'counting the cost', but every commitment in life has a price. When I got married, I promised to 'forsake all others' (not always easy). When I had a child, I gave up going out whenever I fancied. Whatever the individual price we pay for following Jesus, in family loyalty, social status or lifestyle, we need to make our commitment with open eyes. But there is a paradox here: discipleship costs everything, but God's grace is both free and priceless.

PRAYER

'O let me see thy footmarks and in them plant my own; my hope to follow duly is in thy strength alone' (John Ernest Bode, 1816–74).

LOST TREASURE?

LUKE 15:1–4, 8–10 (ABRIDGED)

Now all the tax-collectors and sinners were coming near to listen to him. And the Pharisees and the scribes were grumbling and saying, 'This fellow welcomes sinners and eats with them.'

So he told them this parable: 'Which one of you, having a hundred sheep and losing one of them, does not leave the ninety-nine in the wilderness and go after the one that is lost until he finds it? ...

Or what woman having ten silver coins, if she loses one of them, does not light a lamp, sweep the house, and search carefully until she finds it? When she has found it, she calls together her friends and neighbours, saying, "Rejoice with me, for I have found the coin that I had lost." Just so, I tell you, there is joy in the presence of the angels of God over one sinner who repents.'

Last night I was helping at a church-run soup kitchen. Our 'guests' are a mixed bunch: alcoholics, drug abusers, the mentally ill, two elderly 'military gents', the odd lonely old lady. Yesterday a young man was telling his success story: he'd got a housing offer, a girlfriend and hopes of a job. 'I'm getting my life sorted out,' he said.

I haven't seen any dramatic conversions, but I suspect there's still rejoicing in heaven over the few who make it back to a stable life, for 'the Son of Man came to seek out and to save the lost' (Luke 19:10). Yet those words were addressed not to a street dweller, but to a rich, if corrupt, tax collector named Zacchaeus. God may have a very different idea from ours about who is lost: it may be the people we see in the pages of celebrity magazines or the company director with a 'fat cat' salary.

In these two 'lost and found' stories, the common factor is that the lost item is valuable: the sheep represented potential income, and the coin was probably one of a set, hung on a wedding head-dress as a 'nest egg'.

Business thinking might say that you should write off a small percentage of your assets rather than risk the majority. But God is not a capitalist and will not willingly lose even the least human treasure.

PRAISE

'I once was lost, but now am found' (John Newton, 1725–1807). If this is true for you, praise God.

71

LITTLE BOY LOST

LUKE 15:11–16

Then Jesus said, 'There was a man who had two sons. The younger of them said to his father, "Father, give me the share of the property that will belong to me." So he divided his property between them. A few days later the younger son gathered all he had and travelled to a distant country, and there he squandered his property in dissolute living. When he had spent everything, a severe famine took place throughout that country, and he began to be in need. So he went and hired himself out to one of the citizens of that country, who sent him to his fields to feed the pigs. He would gladly have filled himself with the pods that the pigs were eating; and no one gave him anything.'

Ed and I made our wills when our son was born. Imagine if John, at 18, were to come to us and say, 'Can you please make over the house and capital to me now?' It would be just like saying, 'Mum, Dad, I can't wait for you to die.' In the ancient Middle East it was worse, for grown sons did not leave the family home but stayed and worked for their father. My Muslim friends still tend to do the same.

I expect the listening Pharisees clucked with approval as Jesus outlined the fate of the wayward son. At last, Jesus was punishing a sinner in one of his stories. With the unclean foreigners and their unclean animals was just where this ungrateful youth belonged.

But there's something wrong in the tone of this story. Somehow, subtly, we are being encouraged to sympathize with the hungry, broke young man in his plight. Surely the storyteller isn't going to rescue this one, too?

You know the end, of course, but just for once, let's pretend we don't. Can we put ourselves, in imagination, in the situation of the down-and-out, the young offender terrified and alone in his cell, the teenage girl runaway who is approached by an older man with money? And then can we imagine ourselves in the place of the worried, hurt parent desperate for a phone call—or of the God who loves all these people passionately?

REFLECTION

'A voice is heard in Ramah, lamentation and bitter weeping. Rachel is weeping for her children' (Jeremiah 31:15).

72

LITTLE BOY FOUND

LUKE 15:17–20

'But when he came to himself he said, "How many of my father's hired hands have bread enough and to spare, but here I am dying of hunger! I will get up and go to my father, and I will say to him, 'Father, I have sinned against heaven and before you; I am no longer worthy to be called your son; treat me like one of your hired hands'." So he set off and went to his father. But while he was still far off, his father saw him and was filled with compassion; he ran and put his arms around him and kissed him.'

A famous misprint of this passage reads, '… he ran and put his arms round him and killed him.' That might be the response that many of us expect, and probably the one the listening Pharisees expected! We've all seen the relieved but furious mother shouting her head off at the lost toddler—'Where on earth have you been?'—instead of rejoicing that he's been found.

For the father to hitch up his skirts and run was against all decorum. His other actions are even more extravagant: putting the best robe on his son, a sign of honour; adding a ring, an emblem of authority, and sandals, to show that he was not a barefoot slave; and finally slaughtering the calf he'd been saving so that the whole household can have a roast dinner.

How well do we take this in as a picture of God's attitude to us? In our hymns and prayers, we often still place God on a throne, 'in light inaccessible hid from our eyes' (as the hymn 'Immortal, invisible' puts it), and approach him in fear and trembling. The 'hired hand' that the son asked to become was less secure than a slave: he was engaged by the day and could be sacked at a moment's notice.

Do we fear that God might do the same with us if we put a foot wrong?

The father introduced to us by Jesus is scandalously forgiving in his joy that his younger child 'was dead and is alive again... was lost and is found' (v. 24). This God doesn't seem to mind very much about due procedure and reverence: he likes to party! Maybe our church services should sometimes be more like welcome feasts for returned migrants?

REFLECTION

'You are no longer a slave but... an heir' (Galatians 4:7). 'Let us therefore approach the throne of grace with boldness, so that we may receive mercy' (Hebrews 4:16).

73

BIG BOY LOST

LUKE 15:25–29 (ABRIDGED)

'Now his elder son was in the field; and when he came and approached the house, he heard music and dancing. He called one of the slaves and asked what was going on... Then he became angry and refused to go in. His father came out and began to plead with him. But he answered his father, "Listen! For all these years I have been working like a slave for you, and I have never disobeyed your command; yet you have never given me even a young goat so that I might celebrate with my friends."'

In a meditation on this passage, I was asked which character I identified with. I realized that I felt closest to the elder son! It seems so unfair that those who have had their chance to 'live it up' should be welcomed back into the fold with no questions asked, while I have been a Christian since the age of 16, 'kept my nose clean', and never felt that there was much of a party going on for me.

I was standing in the exact position of the Pharisees. They were pious people, and Jesus acknowledged their righteousness. How understandable is their offence when he spends his time not discussing theology with them, but eating and drinking with Gentiles, fraudsters and dubious women?

But, like the elder son, I'd got it all wrong. Did God ever ask his chosen people to 'work like a slave' and never have a knees-up? Not according to Jesus. Instead, the father in the story says expansively, 'Son... all that is mine is yours' (v. 31). The elder son, he implies, had only to ask: 'You do not have, because you do not ask' (James 4:2b). But he never trusted that his father would give. So he resented the lavish gifts to his brother.

The other night, I dreamt that my parents were hosting a Sunday dinner for some of my church friends at their house. Other people kept turning up, saying, 'We heard there was a shared lunch today.' 'No,' I tried to explain, 'this is a private event, invitation only.' But they kept coming... I woke up and thought for a long time.

PRAYER

'Master, I knew that you were a harsh man... so I was afraid, and I went and hid your talent in the ground' (Matthew 25:24–25). Lord, open our eyes to see your risky generosity, and help us to imitate it.

74

DEBT RELIEF

LUKE 16:1–8 (ABRIDGED)

Then Jesus said to the disciples, 'There was a rich man who had a manager, and charges were brought to him that this man was squandering his property. So he summoned him and said to him, "What is this that I hear about you? Give me an account of your management, because you cannot be my manager any longer." Then the manager said to himself, "What will I do, now that my master is taking the position away from me? ..." So, summoning his master's debtors one by one, he asked the first, "How much do you owe my master?" He answered, "A hundred jugs of olive oil." He said to him, "Take your bill, sit down quickly, and make it fifty." Then he asked another, "And how much do you owe?" He replied, "A hundred containers of wheat." He said to him, "Take your bill and make it eighty." And his master commended the dishonest manager...'

I wonder whether this parable has been rather unfortunately attached by Luke to some sayings about money. I'm not sure it's about money at all. Whenever else Jesus talks about a landowner leaving a steward in charge, the landowner stands for God and the steward for the people of Israel. And wherever debt comes up, it is not literal debt but our debt to God.

So here's a suggestion. If the manager is God's people, his squandering clearly refers to the wrong use of God's gifts: a failure, perhaps, to share wealth justly or care for the needy. When the manager is threatened with the loss of his job, this echoes other threats to 'disinherit' God's chosen: 'What then will the owner of the vineyard do to them? He will come and destroy those tenants and give the vineyard to others' (Luke 20:15–16).

The debtors, then, could be those who were seen as being outside God's people. In slashing their debts, the manager frees them to do new business with the rich man—or, in our interpretation, to enter God's kingdom after all.

The meaning of this story then becomes much more hard-hitting than just, 'If you have money, use it to make friends'. Like all the other stories about unexpected guests and surprise welcomes, it is about who is 'in' and who is 'out'. If God's chosen stewards (us) do not act justly, he has many others to choose from.

REFLECTION

'I have other sheep that do not belong to this fold. I must bring them also' (*John 10:16*).

75

AT THE GATE

LUKE 16:19–26 (ABRIDGED)

'There was a rich man who was dressed in purple and fine linen and who feasted sumptuously every day. And at his gate lay a poor man named Lazarus, covered with sores, who longed to satisfy his hunger with what fell from the rich man's table; even the dogs would come and lick his sores. The poor man died and was carried away by the angels to be with Abraham. The rich man also died and was buried. In Hades... he looked up and saw Abraham far away with Lazarus by his side. He called out, "Father Abraham, have mercy on me, and send Lazarus to dip the tip of his finger in water and cool my tongue; for I am in agony in these flames." But Abraham said, "Child, remember that during your lifetime you received your good things, and Lazarus... evil things; but now he is comforted here, and you are in agony. Besides all this, between you and us a great chasm has been fixed."'

Who fixed the 'great chasm'? We might respond, 'God'. But is the gap in death any bigger than the one in life? Although Lazarus lay at his gate, to the rich man he was invisible. Even dogs were more observant.

This is not primarily a story about the afterlife. It is about how we live here. The chasm was created first by the rich man's greed and indifference—attitudes that had eternal consequences. 'Whatever you bind on earth will be bound in heaven, and whatever you loose on earth will be loosed in heaven' (Matthew 18:18). It is too late to change things, even for the man's five living brothers, for 'if they do not listen to Moses and the prophets, neither will they be convinced even if someone rises from the dead' (Luke 16:31). Notice that even after death the rich man's concerns are only for himself and his own.

The gap remains, but in God's eternal plan the positions are reversed. 'Woe to you who are full now, for you will be hungry,' says Luke's addition to the Beatitudes (6:25). In our globalized economy we might apply this to countries, not just to individuals.

'The rich man in his castle, the poor man at his gate, God made them high or lowly and ordered their estate,' said the Victorian hymn 'All things bright and beautiful'. We should know better, and not blame it on God.

PRAYER

Lord, give us eyes to see the hungry and courage to step across the gap.

76

THE GIFT OR THE GIVER?

LUKE 17:11–16

On the way to Jerusalem Jesus was going through the region between Samaria and Galilee. As he entered a village, ten lepers approached him. Keeping their distance, they called out, saying, 'Jesus, Master, have mercy on us!' When he saw them, he said to them, 'Go and show yourselves to the priests.' And as they went, they were made clean. Then one of them, when he saw that he was healed, turned back... prostrated himself at Jesus' feet and thanked him. And he was a Samaritan.

'And the one that turned back was a Palestinian.' How would that version of the story go down in modern Israel? Substitute whatever group is excluded and oppressed in your own country, for the point of the man's nationality was that he would be unwelcome in Judea. He was doubly a outsider, shunned both for his leprosy and his ethnic group.

Yet these lepers—some Jewish, some Samaritan, some perhaps from other Gentile groups (for this was a very mixed area)—have somehow, in their sickness, become a community. They approach Jesus together; no doubt they live together on the edge of the village. Together they call him 'Master'. What has led them to give him this allegiance and place so much trust in him?

For any of them, to make the statutory visit to the priests (Leviticus 14:1–3) would be a long journey, either to Jerusalem or to the Samaritan temple on Mount Gerizim. To do so shows a strong faith in Jesus' words. It is in their obedience that the leprosy sufferers find the wholeness they seek.

Yet only one, 'a foreigner', returns to give thanks. The others could no doubt argue convincingly, 'We were only doing what you said.' But obedience, while vital, is not everything. If life is just a hard slog to follow a set of commands, we have 'lost the plot'. The Samaritan cares more about loving God in Jesus than about going to the priests for examination. He is full of praise for the gift of healing, but more important to him is to recognize where the gift comes from.

Jesus has been talking a great deal about the kingdom, the great feast, the transformation that God gives. It is vital to stress that the central focus of the feast is not the food, but the host.

REFLECTION

'You search the scriptures because you think that in them you have eternal life… Yet you refuse to come to me to have life' (John 5:39–40). What about us?

77

SAFE OR SAVED?

LUKE 17:22–24, 31–33 (ABRIDGED)

Then he said to the disciples, 'The days are coming when you will long to see one of the days of the Son of Man, and you will not see it. They will say to you, "Look there!" or "Look here!" Do not go, do not set off in pursuit. For as the lightning flashes and lights up the sky from one side to the other, so will the Son of Man be in his day... On that day, anyone on the housetop who has belongings in the house must not come down to take them away; and likewise anyone in the field must not turn back... Those who try to make their life secure will lose it, but those who lose their life will save it.'

What do you look forward to most? As he approaches Jerusalem and his coming suffering, Jesus' mind jumps to the far future, when on 'the day of the Lord' everything in the world will be changed and restored. For him, this day, long spoken of by the Old Testament prophets, has become 'the day of the Son of Man', his own enigmatic title.

'The day' is something to long for, yet it is also frightening, for it will overturn everything in which we have found our security. There is never any shortage of people to predict its coming (v. 23), but few live with the readiness it demands. For most, 'as it was in the days of Noah' (v. 26), ordinary life goes on, with its meals, its commerce, its farming and house building, its festivities.

This prophecy brings together the two threads of promise and challenge that have run through our readings in Luke 13—17. Jesus actually gives us very little hard information about his return. He tells us that it will be sudden and dramatic, like lightning; he tells us that 'no one knows about that day or hour' (Matthew 24:36,

NIV), not even himself. Most importantly, when the time comes, it will not be worth even running downstairs to rescue the photo albums or our favourite jewellery. All we own and are attached to is rendered trivial by the 'great deed', as Julian of Norwich put it, that God will bring about to 'make all things new' (Revelation 21:5). So why are we so attached now?

PRAYER

Imagine you are holding in your hands all that is most precious to you. Offer it all to God for safekeeping—and then leave it there.

JOHN 20–21

....

'Isn't it amazing,' remarked my son when he was five, and reading *The Very Hungry Caterpillar* yet again, 'how a caterpillar goes into a cocoon and turns into a butterfly?' This everyday 'resurrection' had stirred his child's sense of wonder at God's creation.

It's the same sense that John wants to stir in the readers of his final chapters—only here it is wonder at God's redemption, or 're-creation'. John tells us more about Jesus' resurrection appearances than any other Gospel writer (although others have stories that he does not include). The resurrection is the greatest of the 'signs' that John is writing to record, signs which, he says, 'are written so that you may come to believe' (20:31).

The risen Jesus has continuity with the Jesus who walked the streets of Jerusalem and the hills of Galilee, who taught in the temple and by the lake, who performed great miracles and talked of his Father with the powerful and with outcasts. The wounds of his crucifixion are still visible and can be touched; he cooks and joins in a meal—he is very much a physical presence. Yet there is also a mystery about how he suddenly appears within locked doors or on a beach where there was no one before. He is, as it were, a bridge between the carpenter of Nazareth and the Lord whom we meet by his Spirit and in his gathered people.

The purpose of his appearances seems to be to lead the disciples from being a frightened, bewildered and guilty little group who had seen their Master die horribly to a confident gathering of men and women who can proclaim that God has defeated sin and death in his Son. Although there is an apparent 'ending' to the Gospel at 20:31, chapter 21 adds a satisfying feeling of completion as Jesus meets his friends back where they started, in Galilee, gathering up and transforming all their life experience to use in the new world he is calling them to build.

We, too, are called by this risen Lord to be built into the kingdom of God, to be part of the continuing story. May we meet in these pages the one whom death could not hold, for in the words of Sydney Carter's 'Lord of the Dance', 'I am the life that'll never ever die.'

78

PEACE, PAIN AND POWER

JOHN 20:19–23

When it was evening on that day, the first day of the week, and the doors of the house where the disciples had met were locked for fear of the Jews, Jesus came and stood among them and said, 'Peace be with you.' After he said this, he showed them his hands and his side. Then the disciples rejoiced when they saw the Lord. Jesus said to them again, 'Peace be with you. As the Father has sent me, so I send you.' When he had said this, he breathed on them and said to them, 'Receive the Holy Spirit. If you forgive the sins of any, they are forgiven them; if you retain the sins of any, they are retained.'

One Easter Sunday I was worshipping in an ancient and beautiful church. At the end, we all turned to face the back and the great doors were flung wide open. Imagine our surprise when we saw thick snow falling outside!

Jesus has risen, the first fruits from the dead, but it is still winter in the disciples' hearts. They huddle for comfort behind locked doors, terrified of facing the same suffering as their Master. When Jesus breaks in, he brings both peace and a reminder of pain. The 'scars that speak of sacrifice' (to use Graham Kendrick's words) are not wiped out by the resurrection. In fact, it is those very wounds that stir the disciples to joy, for this is how they recognize the Jesus they love.

Nor is the peace that he gives something to be cosily hugged inside, for immediately he sends them out, 'as the Father has sent me'. This means being sent into the world's winter, into risk and pain; for 'servants are not greater than their master' (John 15:20). They do not go alone; they have 'another advocate' (John 14:16).

But the power the Holy Spirit gives must be used wisely, for it is through Jesus' disciples, the body of Christ on earth, that people will receive God's forgiveness—or not receive it.

This is a task that we would hardly dare undertake without the Spirit's guidance. The power to withhold forgiveness has been used too freely by the historic church; the power to forgive, perhaps not enough. In a Jesus-shaped ministry, it should be the reverse, for Jesus takes people's sin and pain into himself—and bears the scars.

REFLECTION

'In Christ God was reconciling the world to himself… and entrusting the message of reconciliation to us' (2 Corinthians 5:19).

79

SOMETHING WE HAVE TOUCHED

JOHN 20:24–28

But Thomas... was not with them when Jesus came. So the other disciples told him, 'We have seen the Lord.' But he said to them, 'Unless I see the mark of the nails in his hands, and put my finger in the mark of the nails and my hand in his side, I will not believe.' A week later his disciples were again in the house, and Thomas was with them. Although the doors were shut, Jesus came and stood among them and said, 'Peace be with you.' Then he said to Thomas, 'Put your finger here and see my hands. Reach out your hand and put it in my side. Do not doubt but believe.' Thomas answered him, 'My Lord and my God!'

'Do you believe in infant baptism?' runs the old joke. Answer: 'Believe in it? I've *seen* it!' The word 'believe' has various meanings. I may believe there are beings on other planets, but it will probably make little difference to me. It will make a lot of difference whether I believe my partner—or anyone—loves me. And if I believe passionately in a cause, I may dedicate my life to it.

We should not be too ready to condemn Thomas as 'doubting Thomas'. Belief that makes a difference is always based on experience. Without any evidence, we would be no different from the rough sleeper who shared my lunch and told me he was Italian royalty.

What Thomas wants is the touch of reality. He wants to feel his Saviour's wounds because that's how he will feel his Saviour's love. We, as the church, owe this reality to any seeker for the truth. 'Sir,' said some truth-seeking Greeks to Philip, 'we wish to see Jesus' (John 12:21). Can we show him in our midst?

So why does Jesus go on to praise those who believe without

seeing (v. 29)? I don't think he is saying 'the less evidence, the more faith'. But faith must survive when sight is darkened. For all of us, there will come times when the well seems empty, when all the props are withdrawn. If with God's help we can still go on trusting, waiting for the risen Christ to reappear, we are truly blessed.

REFLECTION

'What we have heard, what we have seen with our eyes, what we have looked at and touched with our hands... we declare to you' (1 John 1:1, 3).

80

'HOW SWEET THE NAME...'

JOHN 20:30–31

Now Jesus did many other signs in the presence of his disciples, which are not written in this book. But these are written so that you may come to believe that Jesus is the Messiah, the Son of God, and that through believing you may have life in his name.

In Oscar Wilde's play *The Importance of Being Earnest*, two young women fall in love with (apparently) the same man, simply because his name is Ernest. 'There is something in that name that inspires absolute confidence,' asserts one of them.

When you are in love, there is a special thrill in speaking your loved one's name or hearing others speak it—however plain a name it is. Perhaps that is why God commanded his people not to misuse his name, and why the Jews chose not to use their name for God at all, but simply to say 'the Lord'.

For the Christian, there is a preciousness about the name of Jesus, which may make us wince when we hear it, or 'Christ', used as a curse. This also extends (or should) to hearing it used to justify oppression, hatred or unChristlike teaching and actions. But it is not the name itself we value, whether we call him Jesus, Yeshua or Isa. It is the person behind it. And when I think of him, I sense a depth of life and a well of love that I have only just begun to dip into.

'Lord, to whom can we go?' said Peter when Jesus asked his disciples whether they, like others, would leave him. 'You have the words of eternal life' (John 6:68). John's Gospel is very different from the other three in the stories and teachings it records. But today's reading tells us why John has preserved these traditions: 'that through believing you may have life in his name'. John focuses on the key 'signs of life', the miracles and sayings which demonstrate most clearly that the fullness of God's life is in Jesus. 'What has come into being in him was life, and the life was the light of all people' (John 1:3–4).

PRAYER

Weak is the effort of my heart
And cold my warmest thought,
But when I see thee as thou art,
I'll praise thee as I ought.

Till then I would thy love proclaim
With every fleeting breath,
And may the music of thy name
Refresh my soul in death.
JOHN NEWTON (1725–1807)

81

BACK TO THE FUTURE

JOHN 21:1–3

After these things Jesus showed himself again to the disciples by the Sea of
Tiberias; and he showed himself in this way. Gathered there together were
Simon Peter, Thomas called the Twin, Nathanael of Cana in Galilee, the sons
of Zebedee, and two others of his disciples. Simon Peter said to them, 'I am
going fishing.' They said to him, 'We will go with you.' They went out and got
into the boat, but that night they caught nothing.

I've just returned from a retreat in a beautiful, quiet house with a
fabulous garden, all run by lovely nuns who fed me heartily. It was
a shock to return to a demanding child, a house in need of attention
and a tired, grouchy husband.

When Jesus doesn't reappear in Jerusalem, the disciples can think
of nothing to do but return to their former lives as fishermen in
Galilee. Their transformation into apostles—'As the Father sent me,
so I send you' (John 20:21)—has not yet hit home. Not only are
they not yet people-catchers; they aren't even catching any fish!

But there is something deeper going on underneath. I'm
intrigued by the first chapter of John's Gospel. Unlike the other
Gospel writers, John tells us that before meeting Jesus, some of the
disciples had been followers of John the Baptist. They had left their
fishing business and families and travelled all the way from Galilee
to Judea to see John. But when John points them away from himself
to his cousin Jesus, the first thing Jesus does is to take them back to
Galilee (John 1:43)! It must have seemed a real comedown.

Now John's story goes full circle. Once more the disciples are on
Lake Tiberias, fishing. Matthew tells us that the risen Jesus himself,

via the women, had sent them there (Matthew 28:10). If the spread of the gospel is to start from Jerusalem (Acts 1:8), why does he first take them back to their northern roots?

I don't know, but here's a possibility: when God calls us, he doesn't reject our history and background, or the circumstances in which we met him. He begins instead to transform them, to use them for his kingdom. God's economy is lavish, risk-taking, unstinting—but nothing is wasted in it.

REFLECTION

'God knows well how to ride the lame horse and carve the rotten stick'
(Martin Luther, 1483–1546).

82

HIDE AND SEEK

JOHN 21:4–7

Just after daybreak, Jesus stood on the beach; but the disciples did not know that it was Jesus. Jesus said to them, 'Children, you have no fish, have you?' They answered him, 'No.' He said to them, 'Cast the net to the right side of the boat, and you will find some.' So they cast it, and now they were not able to haul it in because there were so many fish. That disciple whom Jesus loved said to Peter, 'It is the Lord!' When Simon Peter heard that it was the Lord, he put on some clothes, for he was naked, and jumped into the sea.

It always seems comical to me that Simon Peter here puts his clothes *on* to jump in the water. Why? Maybe there's a clue in Luke's story of Simon's original calling (Luke 5:1–11). After borrowing Simon's boat to speak from, Jesus tells him to let down his nets—even though he has caught nothing all night. The catch is then so heavy that the nets threaten to break. Simon's reaction is to fall on his knees, begging Jesus to leave him. Somehow God's generosity has made him painfully aware of his own sinfulness.

This later incident must have reminded Peter forcefully of the earlier miraculous marine harvest. Stripped for work, he suddenly feels shamefully exposed, and attempts to cover himself as Adam and Eve did in the garden ('I was afraid, because I was naked; and I hid myself', Genesis 3:10).

It is possible to seek Jesus and at the same time try to hide from him. We want to serve him, to receive his gifts of peace and life, but we are not sure we want him to see too far into the murky recesses of our hearts. This is, of course, futile; he knows it all anyway. If we don't want to be embarrassed by the naked truth, there is only one remedy: 'put on the Lord Jesus Christ' (Romans 13:14). This is a dressing-up game we can all play, for 'as many of you as were baptized into Christ have clothed yourself with Christ' (Galatians 3:27). Like the little girl trying on her mother's dress and shoes, we will need to grow into these new garments, but that, too, is God's work.

PRAYER

Nothing in my hand I bring,
Simply to thy cross I cling;
Naked, come to thee for dress;
Helpless, come to thee for grace.
AUGUSTUS TOPLADY (1740–78)

83

REAL FOOD

When they had gone ashore, they saw a charcoal fire there, with fish on it, and bread. Jesus said to them, 'Bring some of the fish that you have just caught.' So Simon Peter went aboard and hauled the net ashore, full of large fish, a hundred and fifty-three of them; and though there were so many, the net was not torn. Jesus said to them, 'Come and have breakfast.'

A friend was explaining why she valued her boyfriend. 'It's the little things he does,' she said, 'like when he made some bread and honey and brought me it.' Food is a sign of love for most of us—I don't think it's just confined to Jewish mothers like mine! ('Have some more…')

This beach barbecue breakfast is one of the most enticing stories in the New Testament. I can just taste that pungent grilled 'St Peter fish' and freshly charcoal-baked pitta bread. If we have so far seen a rather mindboggling risen Jesus who apparently walks through locked doors, we meet here a very down-to-earth Saviour who certainly thinks real men can cook.

But of course, as always in John, there are deeper meanings. As Jesus handed out the bread and fish, there must have been memories of the extraordinary feeding of five thousand, and of that last meal together when he said, 'This is my body… this is my blood.' And then there were all the other meals, at houses of Pharisees and of tax collectors, and all the stories he told about God's great feast to come. Eating with rich and poor, with the respectable and the outcast, was a hallmark of Jesus' ministry.

Here, as with the little boy's five loaves and two fish (John

6:1–13), he takes what his disciples have and adds it to what he has already provided himself. It is, of course, all provided by God's power, for it is only at his word that they have caught all this fish. We could all witness to how Jesus feeds us spiritually, but often that feeding is expressed in very everyday ways, through actual physical provision—whether it be food, clothing, shelter or hugs. 'My flesh is true food and my blood is true drink' (John 6:55)—not just 'pie in the sky'.

REFLECTION

'He has filled the hungry with good things, and sent the rich away empty'
(Luke 1:53).

84

SHEPHERD TO SHEPHERD

JOHN 21:15–17

When they had finished breakfast, Jesus said to Simon Peter, 'Simon son of John, do you love me more than these?' He said to him, 'Yes, Lord; you know that I love you.' Jesus said to him, 'Feed my lambs'. A second time he said to him, 'Simon son of John, do you love me?' He said to him, 'Yes, Lord; you know that I love you.' Jesus said to him, 'Tend my sheep.' He said to him the third time, 'Simon son of John, do you love me?' Peter felt hurt because he said to him the third time, 'Do you love me?' And he said to him, 'Lord, you know everything; you know that I love you.' Jesus said to him, 'Feed my sheep'.

It's difficult to eat a relaxed, intimate meal with someone with whom you have unresolved conflict. The food tends to stick in your throat. I wonder if that's how Peter felt as he ate breakfast with his beloved rabbi, whom just weeks earlier he had denied knowing. He had to make things right. But how?

With supreme sensitivity, Jesus does it for him. The betrayal is never mentioned, but the threefold questioning clearly echoes the three times the bystanders at Jesus' trial had asked Peter, 'Aren't you one of this man's friends?' and Peter had angrily answered, 'I don't even know him' (see Luke 22:57).

English translations obscure the subtleties in the original Greek. In his first two questions Jesus uses the word *agape*, self-sacrificing love; but Peter answers with *philia*, friendship. The third time, Jesus picks this up and asks, in effect, 'Are you even my friend?' Hence Peter's hurt feelings.

Yet there is an undertone of affection in the questioning: taking the relationship back to its beginnings, Jesus calls him not Peter but (as we would say) 'Simon Johnson'. It's the exasperated yet loving way we might use someone's whole name when they have done something really silly, yet we want to show we still love them.

More than that, Jesus then reaffirms his role as Peter, 'the rock', by renewing his leadership role. He speaks as the good shepherd to an assistant shepherd, giving him responsibility and trusting him to fulfil it. This is true restoration, and it is available to all of us.

PRAYER

Imagine that Jesus is asking you the question he asked Peter. Reply as honestly as you can. Then be silent for his answer.

85

BEYOND THE LAST PAGE

JOHN 21:20–22, 24–25 (ABRIDGED)

Peter turned and saw the disciple whom Jesus loved following them... When Peter saw him, he said to Jesus, 'Lord, what about him?' Jesus said to him, 'If it is my will that he remain until I come, what is that to you? Follow me!' ...

This is the disciple who is testifying to these things and has written them, and we know that his testimony is true. But there are also many other things that Jesus did; if every one of them were written down, I suppose that the world itself could not contain the books that would be written.

Go into the average Christian bookshop and you may be over-whelmed by the sheer volume of titles, let alone the gadgets, stickers and posters with Bible texts on them.

John's speculation on 'the books that would be written' has come true beyond anything he could have imagined. But then the 'things that Jesus did' have, by his Spirit, multiplied way beyond the three years of ministry that John knew about. Each of us could probably write our own book of witness to God's activity.

The continuing story is written in the lives of those who obey the command to 'follow me'. But we all, like Peter, sometimes look to others' lives as a source of speculation and gossip rather than as an example of God's power and grace. Perhaps there's a kind of rivalry going on: Peter has been told 'the kind of death by which he would glorify God' (v. 19) and he may want to know if his friend (very probably John himself) will have the 'honour' of martyrdom as well. Jesus firmly redirects him to what really matters: it is our own lives we are supposed to examine, not those of others.

If you were planning to write an account of how God has acted in your own life and that of your church, what major events and changes would you include? The bookshop shelves may already be full but there is always room in the street, the workplace, the school, even the retirement home, for each of us to 'tell the story' of how God is redeeming his world.

REFLECTION

'You are a letter of Christ… written not with ink but with the Spirit of the living God, not on tablets of stone but on tablets of human hearts' (2 Corinthians 3:3).

ACTS 6—10:
THE WIDENING CIRCLE

It's confession time! For years, I disliked the book of Acts. I could never quite believe that this account of missionary work was written by the same author as the Gospel of Luke, which is my favourite Gospel.

Gradually I realized that my feelings about Acts originated in the way it had been preached to me. Always, when I had heard sermons on Acts, there had been a sort of 'hidden message', intentional or not, which went something like 'Why can't you be more like Paul, you load of miserable failures!' (A bit like the way army sergeants 'encourage' their raw recruits.)

But was there another way of reading Acts? When I found I was required to write Bible reading notes on this book, I determined that I was going to find one. As I progressed, I found that the interests of the Luke who wrote the Gospel could also be found in his second book, if you only looked hard enough. Those interests include the calling and ministry of women, the call to the poor and socially marginalized, the inclusiveness of God's kingdom, and the daring, innovative work of the Holy Spirit.

Finding these emphases in Acts, I began to like it a lot more. It's a book about how the kingdom of God, announced by Jesus, grows from a small group of disciples to a worldwide movement, changing the lives of those who enter it and changing the rules of the society they live in. It's like a wild fairground ride, in which we may some-times feel scared at how fast and far we are being whirled round— but which is still the most exciting ride of our lives.

No wonder, when I was in labour with my son and had inhaled too much gas and air, I found myself muttering, 'I've been all the way from Derbe to Lystra' (we'd had Paul's missionary journeys the previous day in church). The story of Acts is a bit like childbirth: sometimes painful, sometimes confusing, but the beginning of a total change in our lives. The difference is, it's the church, not a baby, that is being born here.

86

NO SECOND-CLASS CITIZENS

ACTS 6:1–4

Now during those days, when the disciples were increasing in number, the Hellenists complained against the Hebrews because their widows were being neglected in the daily distribution of food. And the twelve called together the whole community of the disciples and said, 'It is not right that we should neglect the word of God in order to wait at tables. Therefore, friends, select from among yourselves seven men of good standing, full of the Spirit and of wisdom, whom we may appoint to this task, while we, for our part, will devote ourselves to prayer and to serving the word.'

While recovering from a severe depression, I sewed a tapestry on a circular canvas, making up the design as I went along. I started at the centre with a small 'splatter' of bright red; as I added shapes and colours, it became a glorious outburst of colour radiating from middle to edges.

The movement of Luke's second book reminds me of that tapestry. Jesus promises that the apostles will be his witnesses 'in Jerusalem, in all Judea and Samaria, and to the ends of the earth' (1:8). The movement begins at Pentecost with the apostles' speech being miraculously heard in their native languages by Jews from all over the Roman empire (2:8–11).

But before the gospel can spread freely, one thing must be clear. The Jews of Palestine, to whom Jesus first came, have no special privileges. The Hellenists (Greek-speaking Jews born outside Palestine) must not be treated as second-class citizens; nor must anyone else.

Notice how the apostles address the problem. Recognizing their own special ministry, they do not even take on themselves the task of selecting others to deal with the matter. Instead, they delegate the choice to the gathered church, giving only the most basic guidance: for this practical task, just as for spiritual leadership, the Holy Spirit's wisdom is essential.

It is the community themselves who come up with a suitable list—all of Greek-speaking origin. The church is able to recognize those with the gifts and background appropriate to its needs. Is this true in your church, too? Or do you leave everything to the 'experts'?

REFLECTION

'Now there are varieties of gifts, but the same Spirit; and there are varieties of services, but the same Lord; and there are varieties of activities, but it is the same God who activates all of them in everyone' (1 Corinthians 12:4–6).

87

DANGEROUS WITNESS

ACTS 6:8–12, 15 (ABRIDGED)

Stephen, full of grace and power, did great wonders and signs among the people. Then some of those who belonged to the synagogue of the Freedmen… stood up and argued with Stephen. But they could not withstand the wisdom and the Spirit with which he spoke. Then they secretly instigated some men to say, 'We have heard him speak blasphemous words against Moses and against God.' They stirred up the people as well as the elders and the scribes; then they suddenly confronted him, seized him, and brought him before the council… And all who sat in the council looked intently at him, and they saw that his face was like the face of an angel.

Stephen has already been marked out as 'full of faith and the Holy Spirit' when he was chosen to serve the Greek-speaking widows (6:5). Now the story of his fate as the first Christian martyr draws deliberate parallels between his trial and that of Jesus. The false witnesses claim he said 'that this Jesus of Nazareth will destroy [the temple] and will change the customs that Moses handed on to us' (v. 14). The charges echo those made against his Lord: 'We heard him say, "I will destroy this temple that is made with hands, and in three days I will build another, not made with hands"' (Mark 14:58).

In one sense, the charges are true. Jesus' coming does put an end to all human attempts to appease a demanding God by elaborate systems of religion practised in special places. The temple and all that it represents (religious hierarchy, state-sponsored pomp and circumstance) is redundant in the face of the new 'temple' that Jesus has created: his body, the people who love and follow him.

This, however, is too threatening for the temple authorities, who stand to lose both power and money. Having identified their own establishment with the will of God, they can only see Stephen's witness as 'words... against God'.

It is only too easy for the 'comfortable' part of the world today, even those parts of it that bear the label 'Christian', to label anything that threatens its power base as 'ungodly'. The 'wisdom and the Spirit' displayed by witnesses like Stephen are no more popular today, but the 'face of an angel' is still recognizable—to those who want to see it.

PRAYER

Jesus, help us to hear those who witness to your truth—whoever they are.

88

TAKE IT FROM HERE

ACTS 7:1–5, 8 (ABRIDGED)

Then the high priest asked him, 'Are these things so?' And Stephen replied: 'Brothers and fathers, listen to me. The God of glory appeared to our ancestor Abraham when he was in Mesopotamia... and said to him, "Leave your country and your relatives and go to the land that I will show you." Then he left the country of the Chaldeans and settled in Haran. After his father died, God had him move from there to this country in which you are now living. He did not give him any of it as a heritage... but promised to give it to him as his possession and to his descendants after him, even though he had no child... And so Abraham became the father of Isaac... and Isaac became the father of Jacob, and Jacob of the twelve patriarchs.'

Have you ever had to defend yourself in court, or in any situation where you were accused of something? Maybe you watch courtroom dramas on television. Then you may have noticed that the best defence lawyers start by getting the jury on the defendant's side, arousing their sympathies.

Stephen has been accused of 'blasphemous words against Moses and God' (6:11). The two seem to be identified in his accusers' minds: their image of God is intimately tied up with their history, above all their liberation under Moses. So Stephen begins his defence by retelling the Jewish history of revelation. He is both demonstrating that he knows the scriptures and guaranteeing that his hearers will listen, at least at first, without getting 'turned off'.

Present-day listeners to our defence of the gospel will not be impressed with an opening like 'The Bible says...'. Most will know little of the Bible; it may seem like a collection of irrelevant old stories or a list of 'Thou shalt not's.

To start where *our* hearers are, we have to understand what their image of God is and where they find spiritual meaning. Before we can correct untrue ideas, we may need to affirm what is good in their beliefs. Evangelism seldom prospers by disagreement.

Above all, we must remember that we never 'bring' God to anyone, nor can we 'bring' them to God. God is active everywhere and may already be speaking to our friends; our task is to help them to hear that voice.

PRAYER

Holy Spirit, teach me to witness to my friends, starting from what they already know of you.

89

UNWELCOME PROPHET

ACTS 7:17–29 (ABRIDGED)

'But as the time drew near for the fulfilment of the promise that God had made to Abraham, our people in Egypt increased and multiplied until another king who had not known Joseph ruled over Egypt. He dealt craftily with our race and forced our ancestors to abandon their infants so that they would die. At this time Moses was born, and he was beautiful before God... and when he was abandoned, Pharaoh's daughter adopted him and brought him up as her own son...

When he was forty years old, it came into his heart to visit his relatives, the Israelites. When he saw one of them being wronged, he defended the oppressed man and avenged him... The next day he came to some of them as they were quarrelling and tried to reconcile them... But the man who was wronging his neighbour pushed Moses aside, saying, "Who made you a ruler and a judge over us? Do you want to kill me as you killed the Egyptian yesterday?" When he heard this, Moses fled and became a resident alien in the land of Midian.'

If you are married like me, or even if you have any family or friends, you will be accustomed to introducing sensitive subjects gently! Stephen has got the audience on his side by talking about Abraham and his descendants, then Joseph and his exile, and now the great hero, Moses. Now he must start on the 'bad news': the very people that Moses was sent to rejected him. This will prepare the way for Stephen to show how they have rejected the greatest of prophets, Jesus.

As he goes on, he will accuse the people of having rejected every prophet God ever sent—a charge that recalls Jesus' parable of the tenants in the vineyard, who killed every messenger and eventually even the owner's own son (Matthew 21:33–41). But for now Stephen concentrates on stories that the people know well and accept.

In telling the story of Jesus, whether in an organized evangelistic setting or just informally to friends, how do we balance the good news with the 'bad'? At some point, everyone must discover how much in them is hostile to God's way. We need great wisdom in how we introduce this idea. We must neither wound further those already hurt nor leave the complacent untouched.

REFLECTION

The gospel is meant to comfort the disturbed and disturb the comfortable. Only God can show us which is which.

90

REWRITING HISTORY

ACTS 7:35–40 (ABRIDGED)

'It was this Moses... whom God now sent as both ruler and liberator through the angel who appeared to him in the bush. He led them out, having performed wonders and signs in Egypt, at the Red Sea, and in the wilderness for forty years. This is the Moses who said to the Israelites, "God will raise up a prophet for you from your own people as he raised me up." He is the one who was in the congregation in the wilderness... and he received living oracles to give to us. Our ancestors were unwilling to obey him; instead, they pushed him aside, and in their hearts they turned back to Egypt, saying to Aaron, "Make gods for us who will lead the way for us; as for this Moses who led us out from the land of Egypt, we do not know what has happened to him."'

Every nation has a moment in its history regarded as its 'finest hour'. The older ones among us love to recall past heroism and shake their heads over how far we have fallen since then.

For the Jewish people, the 'finest hour' was, and still is, when God gave Moses the law on Mount Sinai. There they became truly God's people, their identity based on the moral and religious laws of which they were so proud. Just two days ago, I heard a Jewish philosopher suggest that anti-Semitism sprang from anger at the Jews holding up an ideal that no one could live up to.

Stephen, however, has an discomfiting reminder for his people: right from the start they were tempted to abandon their uniqueness, to want to be 'like the nations' (see Ezekiel 20:32). They wanted to worship what they could see and touch rather than the mysterious God of Moses, to ensure the favour of the gods by making sacrifices to all of them.

The direction of Stephen's argument is clear. Just as God's people rejected Moses ('Who made you a ruler and judge?'), so they have now rejected Jesus, whose coming Moses predicted. I imagine it was at this point in Stephen's speech that many hackles rose: nothing angers those attached to a 'glorious' past as much as suggesting that their own role in it was not so glorious.

PRAYER

Lord of history, when I or others try to justify ourselves by our past, remind us that we were sinners then just as now. Only your future kingdom is sin-free.

91

NO EARS TO HEAR

ACTS 7:51–58 (ABRIDGED)

'You stiff-necked people, uncircumcised in heart and ears, you are for ever opposing the Holy Spirit, just as your ancestors used to do. Which of the prophets did your ancestors not persecute? They killed those who foretold the coming of the Righteous One, and now you have become his betrayers and murderers. You are the ones that received the law... and yet you have not kept it.'

When they heard these things, they became enraged and ground their teeth at Stephen. But filled with the Holy Spirit, he gazed into heaven and saw the glory of God and Jesus standing at the right hand of God. 'Look,' he said, 'I see the heavens opened and the Son of Man standing at the right hand of God!' But they covered their ears, and with a loud shout all rushed together against him. Then they dragged him out of the city and began to stone him.

Did Saul, who watched and guarded coats as Stephen was killed, get his idea of the 'circumcised heart' from Stephen's testimony? (see Romans 2:28–29). Certainly something powerful entered his unconscious mind; for at the time 'Saul approved of their killing him' (Acts 8:1), yet later the seed that Stephen had sown would bear fruit in Saul's dramatic experience of the risen Jesus.

'Circumcision of the heart' begins with 'circumcision of the ears', an image that speaks of openness, readiness to hear what may be painful but which can transform us if we let it sink deep into our heart. Stephen's hearers covered their ears, however, and joined in the shout that united them into a savage mob.

As human beings, we are still only too ready to cover our ears or eyes to the fellow humanity of those we don't want to listen to. The people of Nazi Germany (with heroic exceptions) covered their ears to the cries of Jews and other victims of government violence. The killers of black teenager Stephen Lawrence must have covered their ears to his screams as they beat him to death for the 'crime' of being a different ethnic group.

'And Saul approved...' How often do the religious élite (Saul was a leading rabbi) fail to speak against oppression and persecution? Thank God there are always dissenting voices who recognize God's image in every human being. 'Those who have ears, let them hear' (Matthew 11:15, NIV).

REFLECTION

'O that today you would listen to his voice! Do not harden your hearts'
(Psalm 95:7b–8a).

92

THE SALT IS SCATTERED

ACTS 8:1–8 (ABRIDGED)

That day a severe persecution began against the church in Jerusalem, and all except the apostles were scattered throughout the countryside of Judea and Samaria. Devout men buried Stephen and made loud lamentation over him. But Saul was ravaging the church by entering house after house; dragging off both men and women, he committed them to prison.

Now those who were scattered went from place to place, proclaiming the word. Philip went down to the city of Samaria and proclaimed the Messiah to them. The crowds with one accord listened eagerly to what was said by Philip, hearing and seeing the signs that he did... So there was great joy in that city.

I never realized before what a humorous book Acts is! Some have called it 'The Acts of the Holy Spirit', but I wonder whether 'The Jokes of the Holy Spirit' might be equally appropriate. It is full of ironies, of God turning people's plans upside down in the building of the kingdom.

We have just seen a painful irony as the people, incensed at Stephen's charge that they always kill prophets, responded by doing exactly that. Now there is a joyful irony as the persecution spearheaded by Saul has exactly the opposite effect to that intended. Forced to flee Jerusalem, the Christians begin to take the gospel to 'the provinces'.

The outward movement begins, as Jesus prophesied in Acts 1:8, with Judea and Samaria. The Samaritans were the mixed-race survivors of the northern kingdom destroyed by Assyria, who were despised as 'not true Jews' by the Judeans. Philip brings hope and healing to this underclass. So we might say that Saul is already exercising his ministry of taking the gospel to those outside Judaism, even before he knows Jesus for himself! (Notice that both men and women are arrested; later he will call both equally to God's service.)

Jesus told his disciples that they were salt for the earth (Matthew 5:13): without their influence it would be tasteless and rotten. But to do its work, salt must be scattered throughout the food. When we gather in church, it is only to regain our flavour so that we may be effective when scattered in our weekday life.

REFLECTION

'I have other sheep that do not belong to this sheepfold. I must bring them also, and they will listen to my voice' (John 10:16). Meditate on this saying of Jesus, asking him to show you the 'other sheep' he calls you to bring.

93

NOT FOR SALE

ACTS 8:14–20 (ABRIDGED)

Now when the apostles at Jerusalem heard that Samaria had accepted the word of God, they sent Peter and John to them. The two went down and prayed for them that they might receive the Holy Spirit.... Then Peter and John laid their hands on them, and they received the Holy Spirit. Now when Simon saw that the Spirit was given through the laying on of the apostle's hands, he offered them money, saying, 'Give me also this power so that anyone on whom I lay my hands may receive the Holy Spirit.' But Peter said to him, 'May your silver perish with you, because you thought you could obtain God's gift with money!'

When we make friends with those who have no Christian background or commitment, we will encounter values that are radically different from those we learn in church. In reaching out to the Samaritans, the disciples were meeting people who had only partial knowledge of the Jewish faith, and who were inclined to see God in sensational displays of magic tricks. Today's new age spirituality sometimes shows the same tendency.

Simon had been a popular magician, whom the people saw as 'the power of God that is called Great' (8:10). When he was baptized along with many of his former followers, he took along with him a mindset from before his conversion. He watched signs and miracles taking place around Philip and thought that they were simply a fancier version of his own magic. When Peter and John came teaching and demonstrating the gift of the Holy Spirit, he saw the Spirit as the source of all this superior power. Such a power must cost a lot, but it was worth buying.

Peter's shocked reaction is not simply to the mention of money. Simon has radically misunderstood the nature of the Holy Spirit. The Spirit is not a commodity to be bought and sold, a kind of spiritual battery power or certificate of authority to perform certain acts. The Spirit is a person, God with us through the resurrection of Jesus, here to transform individuals and communities 'from one degree of glory into another' (2 Corinthians 3:18). Magic secrets can be passed on for a fee, but miracles are always a free gift.

REFLECTION

'Ho, everyone who thirsts, come to the waters; and you that have no money, come, buy and eat! Come, buy wine and milk without money and without price' (Isaiah 55:1).

94

ON THE ROAD

ACTS 8:26–31 (ABRIDGED)

Then an angel of the Lord said to Philip, 'Get up and go towards the south to the road that goes down from Jerusalem to Gaza.' ... So he got up and went. Now there was an Ethiopian eunuch, a court official of the Candace, queen of the Ethiopians, in charge of her entire treasury. He had come to Jerusalem to worship and was returning home; seated in his chariot, he was reading the prophet Isaiah. Then the Spirit said to Philip, 'Go over to this chariot and join it.' So Philip ran up to it and heard him reading the prophet Isaiah. He asked, 'Do you understand what you are reading?' He replied, 'How can I, unless someone guides me?' And he invited Philip to get in and sit beside him.

When we find a place grim or depressing, we might call it 'godforsaken'. Philip probably thought of the road to Gaza like this. It was a 'wilderness road', with no vegetation, no human habitation, a haunt of wild animals and bandits. It led to a Gentile area, which was always (and still is) seen as a problem by Israel.

Yet this is where the next stage of the gospel's outward spread begins. The eunuch is a 'God-fearer', a Gentile who, as Isaiah prophesied, has come to the 'mountain of Zion' to find wisdom and righteousness (see Isaiah 2:2–3). Not only that, but he is continuing to study the Hebrew scriptures as he travels home.

As a Gentile and a eunuch, the Ethiopian is doubly excluded from the Jewish religion, yet Philip promptly obeys the call to approach him in friendship. As he does, he realizes that this man is, in Jesus' words about another seeker, 'not far from the kingdom of God' (Mark 12:34). No road where someone seeks God is Godforsaken.

Philip's question opens up a conversation without being intrusive or patronizing. He does not rush in with 'answers' until he is invited to do so. An upper-class Ethiopian eunuch and a Greek-speaking Jew (Philip was another of the seven chosen to serve the Greek-speaking widows)—these two might have had every reason to despise and avoid one another. But their mutual desire to follow God makes their meeting a model of respect and courtesy. Do our meetings with those who are different from us measure up?

REFLECTION

'Often, often, often goes Christ in the stranger's guise' (from a Celtic poem).

95

THE WORD IN THE WORDS

ACTS 8:32–35

Now the passage of the scripture that he was reading was this: 'Like a sheep he was led to the slaughter, and like a lamb silent before its shearer, so he does not open his mouth. In his humiliation justice was denied him. Who can describe his generation? For his life is taken away from the earth.' The eunuch asked Philip, 'About whom, may I ask you, does the prophet say this, about himself or about someone else?' Then Philip began to speak, and starting with this scripture, he proclaimed to him the good news about Jesus.

In hospital after giving birth to my son, I read a *New Daylight* comment on this passage. The writer pointed out how poignant his reading must have been for the eunuch, denied the chance to father children, as he read of someone who was unjustly killed before he could leave any offspring. 'Who could have imagined his future?' reads the original verse from Isaiah (53:8) in the NRSV translation. Indeed, we often think of our children as our future, our 'immortality'.

It was poignant for me, too, as I rejoiced in my new baby after years of infertility. Both the eunuch and I could identify with a Jesus who was 'cut off from the land of the living' (Isaiah 53:8), whose life appeared to have borne no fruit.

But the eunuch needed Philip to introduce him to that Jesus, hidden in the scriptures. This meant that Philip had to know how to find him—and I am amazed at how soon people began to discover Jesus in the Hebrew scriptures. Did the couple from Emmaus, who met Jesus on *their* road home, later share what Jesus had explained to them? (Luke 24:25–27).

Perhaps we need to make a double search when we read the Bible—to find our own story in these ancient people's encounters with God, and to find Jesus waiting for us in every part of scripture. Then the words will be the meeting place between our true selves and the living Word of God—in whom we can all be fruitful.

PRAYER

'That you may be filled with the knowledge of God's will in all spiritual wisdom and understanding, so that you may lead lives worthy of the Lord… as you bear fruit in every good work and as you grow in the knowledge of God' (Colossians 1:9–10). Make this your prayer for yourself and your friends.

96

WHO IS THE VICTIM?

ACTS 9:1–5

Meanwhile Saul, still breathing threats and murder against the disciples of the Lord, went to the high priest and asked him for letters to the synagogues at Damascus, so that if he found any who belonged to the Way, men or women, he might bring them bound to Jerusalem. Now as he was going along and approaching Damascus, suddenly a light from heaven flashed around him. He fell to the ground and heard a voice saying to him, 'Saul, Saul, why do you persecute me?' He asked, 'Who are you, Lord?' The reply came, 'I am Jesus, whom you are persecuting.'

Imagine two peoples who had been hostile to each other for centuries. Let's call them the Chalks and the Cheeses. Whom would you choose to lead a peace mission to the Cheeses? A leading Chalk known for his fierce zeal for Chalk culture and religion? Not likely!

Yet for the next stage of the outward reach of the gospel, God does just that. It's another of those 'Jokes of the Holy Spirit': Saul, a Jewish rabbi so aggressively fundamentalist that he leads the persecution of the 'heretical' followers of Jesus—this is the man who will not only be transformed by Jesus but will take his good news to the Gentiles, his traditional enemies.

On the Damascus road, Saul literally 'sees the light': suddenly he perceives that in threatening and hounding Jesus' disciples he is threatening and hounding God himself in Jesus. Although Saul never met Jesus in the flesh, it is the authentic voice of Jesus that he hears: the familiar habit of repeating someone's name when distressed (see Luke 10:41; 22:31), the reminder that the way we treat 'one of these little ones' is the way we treat him (Matthew 25:40, 45).

Saul genuinely thought he was doing the will of God in rooting out this new sect. Only when his eyes are opened to the spiritual reality does he realize that he has been victimizing God himself, in the men and women who are made in God's image. The sad thing is that, so often, those who bear Christ's name have done the same to their fellow Christians.

PRAYER

Think of those who use unjust imprisonment, torture and murder to further their political or religious goals. Make this your prayer for them: 'Father, forgive them, for they do not know what they are doing' (Luke 23:34).

97

ANOTHER CONVERSION

ACTS 9:10–17a (ABRIDGED)

Now there was a disciple in Damascus named Ananias. The Lord said to him in a vision, 'Ananias.' He answered, 'Here I am, Lord.' The Lord said to him, 'Get up and go to the street called Straight, and at the house of Judas look for a man of Tarsus named Saul...' But Ananias answered, 'Lord, I have heard from many about this man, how much evil he has done to your saints in Jerusalem...' But the Lord said to him, 'Go, for he is an instrument whom I have chosen to bring my name before Gentiles and kings and before the people of Israel; I myself will show him how much he must suffer for the sake of my name.' So Ananias went and entered the house.

This chapter is a story of two conversions. The first is that of Saul the persecutor, who will become the great apostle Paul. The second is that of Ananias. Yes, Ananias is already a follower of what was then called the Way, but there is a vital aspect of Jesus' teaching and example that he has still to learn. It is this: 'Love your enemies, do good to those who hate you, bless those who curse you, pray for those who abuse you' (Luke 6:27–28).

When Saul, the church's enemy number one, comes to Ananias for healing of his temporary blindness, Ananias must be ready to lay hands on him in the name of Jesus. Why didn't God heal Saul directly? Because there are two dimensions to every conversion. The first is reconciliation with God; Saul has undergone that on the road. The second is reconciliation with enemies. Without learning love of people as well as love of God, Saul will never be a disciple, let alone an apostle.

I find it very moving that Ananias not only gently touches Saul, but that his first word to him is 'Brother' (v. 17b). What we call people is how we see them. Call someone 'backslider' or 'heretic' and that is how we will treat them. Call them 'sister' or 'brother' and a very different relationship will emerge.

REFLECTION

'For he is our peace; in his flesh he has made both groups into one and broken down the dividing wall, that is, the hostility between us' (Ephesians 2:14). Where have you seen or heard of this happening? Where would you like it to happen? Turn your desire into prayer.

98

INTRODUCING THE NEW BOY

ACTS 9:26–28

When [Saul] had come to Jerusalem, he attempted to join the disciples; and they were all afraid of him, for they did not believe that he was a disciple. But Barnabas took him, brought him to the apostles, and described for them how on the road he had seen the Lord, who had spoken to him, and how in Damascus he had spoken boldly in the name of Jesus. So he went in and out among them in Jerusalem, speaking boldly in the name of Jesus.

In Baptist churches, a new attender may bring a letter from their old church leaders certifying that they are a member 'in good standing' and recommending them for membership of the new church. We all have our ways of introducing new members to a group, some official, some unofficial. (The novel *Tom Brown's School Days*, in its description of 'roasting' a new pupil, shows a rather more brutal way of initiating!)

Saul the persecutor had had letters from the Jerusalem synagogue to the Damascus one, authorizing him to arrest Christians. Now he himself is a target for persecution. Forced to flee back to Jerusalem, he has no official introduction to the church there, for whom he is still the enemy. It is yet another irony: the persecutor is now the victim, the refugee-maker a fugitive.

Barnabas, the 'son of encouragement' (Acts 4:36), is one of the most courageous figures in the New Testament. Taking the role played by Ananias in Damascus, but without a vision like that of Ananias to support him, he meets and welcomes Saul and listens with an open mind to his story. Then he gently presents this new son to the mother church and entrusts him to its care. In response, the Jerusalem believers not only accept Saul but allow him space to exercise his calling: he 'went in and out' like any other sheep of the sheepfold (see John 10:9).

Paul's own account in Galatians 1—2 suggests a rather longer period of 'testing and training' before his ministry was endorsed. In my own church, we have a flexible 'novice' period for potential new members, to make sure they are ready for the commitment of membership. But the principle is the same: whom God has accepted, we reject at our peril.

REFLECTION

'No one can come to me unless drawn by the Father who sent me' (John 6:44a); 'Welcome one another, therefore, just as Christ has welcomed you' (Romans 15:7a).

99

GREATER WORKS?

ACTS 9:36–40

Now in Joppa there was a disciple whose name was Tabitha, which in Greek is Dorcas. She was devoted to good works and acts of charity. At that time she became ill and died. When they had washed her, they laid her in a room upstairs. Since Lydda was near Joppa, the disciples, who heard that Peter was there, sent two men to him with the request, 'Please come to us without delay.' So Peter got up and went with them; and when he arrived, they took him to the room upstairs. All the widows stood beside him, weeping and showing tunics and other clothing that Dorcas had made while she was with them. Peter put all of them outside, and then he knelt down and prayed. He turned to the body and said, 'Tabitha, get up.' Then she opened her eyes, and seeing Peter, she sat up.

I don't know anyone who's been raised from the dead or raised anyone from the dead—do you? One hears stories, but they are always set in Africa or further away.

Jesus certainly prophesied that his disciples would do 'the works that I do' and even greater ones (John 14:12), and this miracle has features that recall Jesus' own miracles: for instance, Peter's sending everyone away, just as Jesus sent away everyone (except James, John and Peter) when he raised Jairus' daughter (Mark 5:35–42). But that very detail also demonstrates that this 'great work' is not just for show.

Tabitha has not been engaged in hobby embroidery. She has been a vital and much-loved member of the 'order of widows', who without their support of each other would have been destitute (their families might have rejected them for following Jesus). Luke's inclusion of her story in Acts shows his special interest in women and the poor, as well as in the Holy Spirit's power. The work she did was essential to the church. They could not afford for her to die.

Our 2000-year-old church may need different 'great works', some of which may be unglamorous and hidden. Anyway, would the world believe 'even if someone rises from the dead'? (Luke 16:30–31). Paul told the Corinthians to 'strive for the greater gifts'—and what was the greatest? Love (1 Corinthians 13).

PRAYER

Does your church value the gifts and ministry of every member—especially the women and the poor? Pray that you will regard each other as irreplaceable.

100

A MOVING STORY

ACTS 10:1-8

In Caesarea there was a man named Cornelius, a centurion of the Italian Cohort, as it was called. He was a devout man who feared God with all his household; he gave alms generously to the people and prayed constantly to God. One afternoon at about three o'clock he had a vision in which he clearly saw an angel of God coming in and saying to him, 'Cornelius.' He stared at him in terror and said, 'What is it, Lord?' He answered, 'Your prayers and your alms have ascended as a memorial before God. Now send men to Joppa for a certain Simon who is called Peter; he is lodging with Simon, a tanner, whose house is by the seaside.' When the angel who spoke to him had left, he called two of his slaves and a devout soldier from the ranks of those who served him, and after telling them everything, he sent them to Joppa.

I've just come back from the Greenbelt Christian music and arts festival, where seminars and workshops explore aspects of our faith and living. One speaker there runs a church that welcomes drug addicts, travellers, bikers, those regarded by 'respectable' people as outcasts. He said that there are really only two sorts of people: those who are moving towards Jesus and those who are moving away from him. Some of the most apparently righteous might in fact be moving away, while the confused, disreputable or broken might be on a journey moving closer to him.

Cornelius, while of high standing in his own Roman society and a 'God-fearer'—in other words, a Gentile disciple of Judaism—was near the lowest rung of the ladder in Jewish eyes. He was only allowed into the outer court of the temple, just a little less far in than Jewish women could go; an area that had been filled up with money changers and animal sellers so that there was no room left to worship.

This second-class follower of Yahweh is about to be called to move in closer. Far from being an outsider with God, he has been noticed and his prayers and service to the poor have been received with joy. Now God will offer him a salvation beyond his wildest dreams. He is ready. The next of the Spirit's strategic moves is to prepare the church to welcome him.

PRAYER

'Father of all, we give you thanks and praise, that when we were still far off you met us in your Son and brought us home' (Service of Holy Communion, Common Worship).

101

THE BREAKTHROUGH

ACTS 10:9–16 (ABRIDGED)

About noon the next day... Peter went up on the roof to pray. He became hungry and wanted something to eat; and while it was being prepared, he fell into a trance. He saw the heaven opened and something like a large sheet coming down, being lowered to the ground by its four corners. In it were all kinds of four-footed creatures and reptiles and birds of the air. Then he heard a voice saying, 'Get up, Peter; kill and eat.' But Peter said, 'By no means, Lord; for I have never eaten anything that is profane or unclean.' The voice said to him again, a second time, 'What God has made clean, you must not call profane.' This happened three times, and the thing was suddenly taken up to heaven.

As a teenage vegetarian, I once absent-mindedly offered an unwanted ham sandwich to a Jewish friend. My choice of recipient was not exactly inspired!

Food laws for the Jews were (and are) both a mark of distinction from other peoples and an effective way of ensuring that people remember God at all times—for we always need to eat. The exclusion of certain foods as 'unclean' was part of a system of clean and unclean practices, objects and people.

Jesus told his shocked disciples that it is not what goes into our mouths that makes us unclean, but what comes out of us (Matthew 15:10–11). I wonder what they thought he meant at first! He explained that out of our mouths comes what is really deepest in us: rage, greed, hatred, lies and lust.

The line between good and evil goes not between different people or between different nations, but right through the centre of the human soul. As James pointed out, blessings and curses can come from the same mouth (James 3:10).

Peter's vision is perhaps the most important breakthrough in the whole history of the Church—not just because it meant that the despised Gentiles could then be admitted (and that includes most of you reading this), but because it abolished for ever, for Christians, the idea that one type or ethnic group of person can be superior to another or more acceptable to God. Not only that, but it established that everything God has made is good, if used rightly. Anyone who claims otherwise is not speaking God's truth.

REFLECTION

Why do you think it is that Christians have sometimes supported racism and discrimination?

102

STEP BY STEP

ACTS 10:19–20, 23–28 (ABRIDGED)

While Peter was still thinking about the vision, the Spirit said to him, 'Look, three men are searching for you. Now get up, go down, and go with them without hesitation; for I have sent them.' ... So Peter invited them in and gave them lodging.

The next day he got up and went with them, and some of the believers from Joppa accompanied him. The following day they came to Caesarea. Cornelius was expecting them and had called together his relatives and close friends. On Peter's arrival Cornelius met him, and falling at his feet, worshipped him. But Peter made him get up, saying, 'Stand up; I am only a mortal.' And... he said to them, 'You yourselves know that it is unlawful for a Jew to associate with or visit a Gentile; but God has shown me that I should not call anyone profane or unclean.'

Why did Peter need the Spirit to tell him that three men were looking for him? After all, they were calling at his gate; surely soon he would hear them, or they would go in and see if anyone was at home! Is Luke over-spiritualizing his story here?

I think not. Luke is always concerned to get his facts right (see Luke 1:1–4). His overwhelming interest, though, is not in factual detail but in how the Holy Spirit steadily moves people on to the next stage. For Peter, to go with the men would be a huge step, so he needs the assurance of the Spirit's guidance first.

I expect you, like me, sometimes get irritated by people claiming, 'The Lord told me...' or 'God gave me this poem' (especially when the poem isn't very good!) We can often use God to justify our own desires—then no one dares question us. Two things strike me in this account. One is that the Spirit's message is confirmed by ordinary people saying ordinary things. The messengers report that they are sent by 'Cornelius... an upright and God-fearing man, who is well spoken of by the whole Jewish nation' (v. 22), all of which helps to convince Peter. Secondly, no one acts alone: Peter takes other believers along; Cornelius gathers his friends and family. This is a clear case of 'It seemed good *to us and to the Holy Spirit*' (Acts 15:28).

REFLECTION

When we get surprising messages, we do well to test them with common sense, with the Christian community—and with the Bible.

103

SEEKERS, FINDERS

ACTS 10:34–43 (ABRIDGED)

Then Peter began to speak to them: 'I truly understand that God shows no partiality, but in every nation anyone who fears him and does what is right is acceptable to him. You know the message he sent to the people of Israel, preaching peace by Jesus Christ—he is Lord of all. That message spread throughout Judea... how God anointed Jesus of Nazareth with the Holy Spirit and with power; how he went about doing good and healing all who were oppressed by the devil, for God was with him... They put him to death by hanging him on a tree; but God raised him on the third day and allowed him to appear... to us who were chosen by God as witnesses... He commanded us to preach to the people and to testify that he is the one ordained by God as judge of the living and the dead. All the prophets testify about him that everyone who believes in him receives forgiveness of sins through his name.'

'Everyone who has heard and learned from the Father comes to me,' said Jesus (John 6:45). Genuine seekers, like Cornelius, will find their way to him—for God is seeking them. The qualifications are simple: 'Whoever would approach him must believe that he exists and that he rewards those who seek him' (Hebrews 11:6).

So if you meet a seeker for truth and goodness, what will you tell them? Peter delivers the whole Jesus story in less than 200 words here: his message, his ministry, his death, resurrection and its results—as well as his role as future judge.

Different church traditions emphasize different aspects of the gospel, and few if any get the balance right. Maybe different people respond to different emphases; we need sensitivity and wisdom to show us where to start. Perhaps the most vital part of Peter's message is in a sentence that I missed out from the passage printed above: 'We are witnesses to all he did' (v. 39). He speaks of 'what we have heard, what we have seen with our eyes, what we have looked at and touched with our hands, concerning the word of life' (1 John 1:1).

Unlike Peter, we have not seen and touched Jesus bodily—or have we? If the church is his body, then what we experience there is experience of him. We are all witnesses, and can tell what we have seen.

REFLECTION

'One thing I do know, that though I was blind, now I see' (John 9:25).

104

IF GOD IS FOR US...

ACTS 10:44–48

While Peter was still speaking, the Holy Spirit fell upon all who heard the word. The circumcised believers who had come with Peter were astounded that the gift of the Holy Spirit had been poured out even on the Gentiles, for they heard them speaking in tongues and extolling God. Then Peter said, 'Can anyone withhold the water for baptizing these people who have received the Holy Spirit just as we have?' So he ordered them to be baptized in the name of Jesus Christ. Then they invited him to stay for several days.

When I was younger, there was much dispute about whether 'baptism in the Spirit' was a second gift following on water baptism, or whether all Christians baptized in the name of Father, Son and Holy Spirit automatically 'had' the Spirit. People appealed to passages like this to support either side, and sometimes the heated debate displayed little evidence of the Spirit's work in the debaters!

Surely the point of today's story is that no one 'has' the Holy Spirit as their private possession. 'The wind blows where it chooses... So it is with everyone who is born of the Spirit' (John 3:8). The Jewish disciples of Jesus thought they had exclusive rights to the Spirit—after all, hadn't Jesus himself said, 'Salvation is from the Jews' (John 4:22)? Their amazement was not at *when* the Spirit came to Cornelius and his family—before baptism—but *where* and *on whom* the gift fell. No doubt they had forgotten that those words about salvation were uttered to an outcast Samaritan woman, to whom Jesus offered living water!

We insecure human beings like to have boundaries defining who is 'in' and who is 'out', but God's Spirit may not have the same categories. Peter's response shows an admirable readiness to recognize what God is doing.

If only we could have some of the same openness in our own churches, how much less the barriers between different traditions would matter! If only we could recognize that wherever people are 'extolling God', the Spirit of God is there (for this, not the speaking in tongues, is the real deciding factor).

When Peter reports this story back to Jerusalem, the Judean believers are silenced with awe. The stage is set for the Jesus movement to reach the whole world—including you and me.

REFLECTION

'If God gave them the same gift... who was I that I could hinder God?' *(Acts 11:17).*

✣

A POOR THING, BUT MINE OWN

Some of the columns in this book date from way back BM, BC and BM (that's Before Marriage, Before Child and Before Mennonites). Having started my Christian life in a medium-sized Baptist church, I became an 'accidental Anglican' at university and stayed one for about ten years after (I even had a shotgun confirmation just days before becoming a churchwarden). This piece dates from those days. One thing I do miss, having left the 'parish system', is the rich social mix described below. However, I still belong to a small, struggling congregation (the only Mennonite church in the UK!) with its share of oddball and difficult people. So maybe things haven't changed that much.

'You must come to my church, it's really good—we get about a thousand on a Sunday morning.' An odd recommendation, I've always thought. A bit like saying, 'Do try this delicious spaghetti, each piece is over three feet long.' Why is a large church automatically assumed to be a good church? Since when has the 'ten million lemmings can't be wrong' principle been a recognized part of Christian thinking? And why, if this marvellous church has a thousand regular worshippers already, should it be so desperately keen to get hold of me as well?

Yet time and again, wherever I meet Christian strangers, I get versions of the invitation above. Even the innocent-sounding question, 'What church do you go to?' conceals an unspoken assumption that it must be somewhere the questioner has heard of—in other words, somewhere big and famous. As soon as they hear the diffident reply, 'Oh, only my local parish church', they can't wait to haul me off to their favoured temple of the preaching arts. It must be good, they have twelve house groups meeting every night.

Well, dear people whom I meet at parties and conferences, I

suppose I should thank you. It's very generous of you to be so concerned for my spiritual welfare. I do realize that by going to a church no one's heard of, I'm putting my Christian life severely at risk. I mean, we can't rely on God to keep me growing, without the help of one of the top ten preachers, can we?

But I'm afraid I have an unconquerable vice. I actually *like* my small, struggling, inner-city church. I don't go there out of a noble sense of vocation, to bestow my valuable services on a needy congregation. I go there because I want to. To tell the truth, nothing makes me feel quite so alienated from God as a congregation of a thousand people. I can only hope that there will be a few little chapels and hermitages reserved in heaven for cranks like myself.

Let me tell you a little about my church, since you've often told me at such length about yours. It's two churches really—at least, there are two buildings and historically two congregations. One is supposedly 'high'—incense, full vestments, the lot. The other has, in the past, prided itself on being 'low' (one former parishioner was heard to remark, 'They're Anglican at the other place, but we're Protestant'). But since we united the two congregations and by general agreement ditched some of the more obvious differences, you'd be hard put to tell which is which. As far as most of us are concerned, we're all just Christians.

'All' means, on a good Sunday, about 30. The church makes a lot of noise these days about strengthening the family, but you won't find many families at ours—not, at any rate, the respectable sort with two parents. It's not that sort of area. You will, however, find just about every other social group and personal situation you can think of.

There's Sid, for instance, who lives in the local Sally Army and spends his days shuffling painfully up and down the street. Sid doesn't drink, but he's what they used to call 'a bit touched'. He turns up faithfully to every church event, especially if there's food laid on. On bad days, all you'll get from him is abuse. On good days, he suddenly launches into surprisingly competent harmonies to whatever hymn we're belting out (you have to belt them out at our place). One of Sid's more unusual traits is a keen interest in ecclesiastical appointments. It can be a bit disconcerting, in the middle of a Bible study, to be asked urgently, 'Who's the bishop of X, then? It used to be Y, didn't it?' But we're used to it by now.

Then there's Eulalie, a West Indian woman who, from a succession of families, has managed to salvage only one small son and no husband either official or unofficial. Eulalie can only just read and willingly accepts help in finding the page in the service book (wouldn't all Anglicans like some occasional help with that). Yet she diligently reads her Authorized Version every day at home and in prayer meetings comes out with obviously heartfelt prayers in an engaging mixture of 17th-century and modern English. Eulalie's very hot on trusting God for everyday needs. On her income as a cleaner, way below the poverty line, she has to be.

There's Dennis, a bachelor who, last year, in his early 70s, finally moved out of the house where he was born—into a flat two minutes round the corner. Now *that's* what I call local. Dennis is a great reader of lessons and belter-out of hymns, and has just retired as churchwarden after 27 years. I only stuck it for three.

There's Fay, who works 24 hours a day to keep together a difficult family, plagued by illness and largely dependent on her income, father being unemployed. Fay leaves early if the sermon's too long: her teenage son has to have his Sunday lunch on time or else.

There's Margaret, who often preaches the long sermons that distress Fay so much. But then she's so eager to see us grow in faith, there's so much she wants to say to us...

There's a sprinkling of worthy widows, an admiral's daughter, a couple of actors, the statutory old lady or two, even the odd Oxbridge graduate. There's me—well, you know something of my shortcomings by now.

Such is the raw material with which God must build the kingdom in one small patch of London. It's not very promising, I admit. We can't chalk up an impressive tally of conversions, and no one would bother to travel more than a few miles to visit us. Yet somehow I can't help feeling proud of this motley bunch. It may be because we've not only survived but been brave enough to take ridiculous risks—like agreeing to a half-million-pound project to develop our crypt as a much-needed day centre for the single homeless. It may be because a recent visitor, treated as an oddity in more conventional churches, observed significantly of ours, 'They didn't look at me as if I were something from outer space.'

But I think it's mainly because we know that we haven't any assets except God himself. If ever our church achieves anything that will register on the Christian 'success scale', it will quite clearly be a miracle. I have a sneaking feeling it *is* a miracle to find Eulalie, Sid, Margaret and myself all worshipping together.

On a worldly view, you might say I've chosen as Shakespeare's Touchstone chose his Audrey: 'A poor virgin, sire, an ill-favoured thing, sire, but mine own; a poor humour of mine, sir, to take that that no man else will' (*As You Like It*). I prefer to borrow the words that Carlo Carretto puts in the mouth of Francis in his imaginative 'autobiography' of the saint:

> *My Church, my church*
> *homely as you are*
> *you are ever my church.*
> I, FRANCIS (ORBIS BOOKS, 1982)

After all, isn't the Bride of Christ everywhere in rags till her bridegroom clothes her?

TIME TO GO

HEAVEN AND HELL

Hanging out washing the other day, I came up with my own image of hell: matching socks for eternity, and always having one left over! Heaven is meeting up with all my old friends at the Greenbelt festival (with more toilets and no rain).

No doubt you have your own pictures of what might lie beyond death. The Bible gives us remarkably little information, so Christians over the millennia have been free to exercise their imaginations. And they have done so liberally, coming up with limbo, purgatory, fallen angels and all sorts of other theories.

In reaction to this, my husband's Christadelphian forebears decided to do away with demons in red tights with pitchforks, and angels in white nighties, and take a hard look at what the Bible actually does say. I think they were right in this, and I have attempted to do the same in these notes. I have, however, explored a little of how the Bible might be interpreted in alternative ways.

Some evangelists love to threaten hell and promise heaven as part of their emotional armoury to get people to listen to Jesus. We've all heard 'fire and brimstone' preaching or seen tracts saying 'Are you sure you'll get to heaven?' It's notable that the early church didn't mention either hell or heaven in its preaching (see Peter's sermon in Acts 2, for example). The first believers were more keen on telling the good news that in Jesus, God's kingdom has come close and you can just walk into it.

We shouldn't be so interested in where we or others are going after death that we forget to live the Jesus life here on earth. We mustn't be 'so heavenly minded that we're no earthly use'. Nor should we indulge in condemning others to hell. Jesus never said that we would be the judges of good and evil, but that 'on the last day the word that I have spoken will serve as judge' (John 12:48).

It is important, though, that we speak that word, and obey it, faithfully. A vision of God's ultimate transformation of this world and the destruction of evil should help motivate us to do that. There is justice in the end. Our work is not in vain (1 Corinthians 15:58).

105

IS THAT ALL?

JOB 19:25–26; PSALM 139:7–8

For I know that my Redeemer lives, and that at the last he will stand upon the earth; and after my skin has been thus destroyed, then in my flesh I shall see God.

Where can I go from your spirit? Or where can I flee from your presence? If I ascend to heaven, you are there; if I make my bed in Sheol, you are there.

On the radio programme *Quote Unquote*, I heard a panellist say that on his mother's grave he planned to put her favourite saying: 'That'll do'. But for many of us—perhaps, deep down, all of us—this brief life won't do. Especially if our life is full of sorrows, or we are very aware of others' suffering, we are bound to ask: is it 'life's a bitch and then you die'? Do I, or those I love, just disappear?

The Hebrew scriptures say very little about an afterlife. The Old Testament talks about 'Sheol', often translated 'the grave' and thought of as a shadowy, mysterious underworld. All the dead went down to it, but no one ever came back to report what it was like.

Yet now and then there are extraordinary glimpses of hope for a future world where wrongs would be put right, eternal questions be answered and humans see God 'face to face'. Job's cry of faith, in the midst of lamenting his ruined life, is one such glimpse. Notice how he speaks of seeing God 'in my flesh'; in Jewish thought, body and soul cannot live independently (that's a Greek idea), but we are a unity of body, mind and spirit. The image of heaven as a realm of disembodied spirits floating about (or hell as disembodied spirits somehow being tormented) is not a biblical one. Job expects to be recognizably Job in God's presence.

The psalmist looks at the same idea from another angle. You might expect to find God in heaven—but in hell? Perhaps we need to rethink our talk of hell as 'separation from God'. There is nowhere in the universe where God is not.

REFLECTION

'My Redeemer lives, and at the last he will stand upon the earth.' Let this thought inspire your worship.

106

HARVEST TIME

LUKE 3:15–17

As the people were filled with expectation, and all were questioning in their hearts concerning John, whether he might be the Messiah, John answered all of them by saying, 'I baptize you with water; but one who is more powerful than I is coming; I am not worthy to untie the thong of his sandals. He will baptize you with the Holy Spirit and fire. His winnowing-fork is in his hand, to clear his threshing-floor and to gather the wheat into his granary; but the chaff he will burn with unquenchable fire.'

In Terry Pratchett's popular *Discworld* novels, Death, the Grim Reaper, speaks in capital letters. John the Baptist reminds me rather of this character. He's a capital letters sort of man.

John's role is to prepare people for the kingdom of God that Jesus will usher in. His way of doing so is to make them aware of their moral and spiritual (and social) failings. This may sound like 'first the bad news', but in fact, the announcement that there will be a 'harvest', in which good will be rewarded and evil destroyed, is good news. It tells us that all the injustices and sufferings of this wounded earth are going to be put right—that God has a day of reckoning for the oppressor and the exploiter.

As well as this, John makes it clear that we are not doomed from birth to be either nutritious wheat or tasteless bran. He offers a way that we can begin to change from bran to wheat: by baptism, a physical 'bath' signifying a spiritual desire to be cleansed and start a new life. Even this, however, is nothing compared to the baptism that Jesus will bring—a baptism that reaches the spiritual parts John's cannot reach!

Finally, John offers a hint of how the New Testament sees heaven and hell. Those who are fit to live with God are gathered into God's 'grain store', to be used to feed the world. The unfit are destroyed completely, because there is no goodness in them. This gathering and destroying starts now—as we will see in the next reading.

REFLECTION

Feeling useless? If you have entered God's kingdom by faith and baptism, you are becoming fruitful grain, and God has a use for you.

107

TWO ROADS

MATTHEW 7:13–14

'Enter through the narrow gate; for the gate is wide and the road is easy that leads to destruction, and there are many who take it. For the gate is narrow and the road is hard that leads to life, and there are few who find it.'

> *Two roads diverged in a wood; and I,*
> *I took the one less travelled by*
> *And that has made all the difference.*

Robert Frost's much-loved poem ('The road not taken') provides the title for M. Scott Peck's bestseller, *The Road Less Travelled*. Peck's book opens with the words, 'Life is difficult.' It is a very Jesus-like sentiment.

We have read how John promised a sorting out of those who were fruitful from those who were mere tasteless, unnourishing 'bran'. But where does this 'great divorce' (to use C.S. Lewis' phrase) start?

In this extract from the collection of teaching known as the Sermon on the Mount, Jesus gives us the image of two roads. The narrow path, with a small gate at its entrance, leads to life—but because it is hard, few people choose it. You can't get through a narrow gate with a lot of baggage (a bit like that camel trying to get through the eye of a needle: Matthew 19:24). The other fork has a nice wide entrance, easy to get through, and the road looks like pleasant, easy walking. No wonder the majority take it; but it leads to destruction.

Of course, most of those who choose the broad road do so by default. We may not even know we have chosen. It is the route of inertia and indifference. The road to hell may not be paved with good intentions so much as with no particular intentions at all.

The two roads hint at an eternal outcome: either life in all its fullness or destruction—being 'unmade'. But this image is not only about 'life after death'. It is about how we choose to live right now, and the impact that that has on all around us.

The roads to heaven and hell begin right here on earth; so do the effects of our choice between them. Real life is difficult; but ultimately, it's the only life there is.

PRAYER

Though our road may be narrow, may our minds never be so.

108

BY THEIR FRUITS

MATTHEW 25:31–36

When the Son of Man comes in his glory, and all the angels with him, then he will sit on the throne of his glory. All the nations will be gathered before him, and he will separate people one from another as a shepherd separates the sheep from the goats, and he will put the sheep at his right hand and the goats at the left. Then the king will say to those at his right hand, 'Come, you that are blessed by my Father, inherit the kingdom prepared for you from the foundation of the world; for I was hungry and you gave me food, I was thirsty and you gave me something to drink, I was a stranger and you welcomed me, I was naked and you gave me clothing, I was sick and you took care of me, I was in prison and you visited me.'

Can you tell sheep from goats? Probably quite easily, as Western sheep and goats look quite different from each other. Middle Eastern sheep, however, are long-haired and look very similar to goats. You have to bring them together to tell the difference.

In this challenging parable, Jesus brings all the people of the earth together to 'compare and contrast' them. This is part of a series of teachings on being ready for the coming kingdom, including the stories of the thief who comes in the night (Matthew 24:42–44), the slave awaiting his master's return (vv. 45–51), the wise and foolish bridesmaids (25:1–13), and the servants given money to invest (vv. 14–30).

Mennonite writer Randy Klassen notes that 'no judgment passage asks anything about the doctrines or beliefs of the individual' (*What Does the Bible Really Say about Hell?* Pandora Press, 2001). In all these stories, the master, bridegroom or Son of Man is looking for those who have faithfully lived up to their calling (even the thief wants tangible goods!).

Catholic tradition calls the actions described here 'the seven works of mercy'. God does not want duty done with gritted teeth, but for us to show the same kindness and compassion that God has shown us.

We are not saved by belief, but by grace. Faith is the way we come to live under grace. That grace is the foundation of everything good we do.

REFLECTION

Have you met Jesus in the needy recently?

109

SCARY STORIES

MATTHEW 8:11–12; MARK 9:47–48

'I tell you, many will come from east and west and will eat with Abraham and Isaac and Jacob in the kingdom of heaven, while the heirs of the kingdom will be thrown into the outer darkness, where there will be weeping and gnashing of teeth.'

'And if your eye causes you to stumble, tear it out; it is better for you to enter the kingdom of God with one eye than to have two eyes and to be thrown into hell, where their worm never dies, and the fire is never quenched.'

Do you know the story of the preacher speaking on eternal torment, dwelling especially on the gnashing of teeth? 'I haven't got any teeth,' piped up an old man. 'Teeth,' intoned the preacher, 'will be provided.'

Jesus speaks often of judgment, usually with frightening imagery. Many preachers and teachers have taken this literally, and put 'the fear of God' into their audiences. Medieval churches had wall paintings of the torments of hell—the 'horror films' of their day. Were they right?

We need to look at some New Testament background. Jesus uses two words for hell: the Greek *Hades*, but more commonly the Hebrew *Gehenna* (used in today's reading from Mark). The word came from the valley of Hinnom, south of Jerusalem. Here, in pagan times, children were burned in sacrifice to Moloch. Later it was a refuse tip and the bodies of the worst criminals were dumped there. So the fire was continually burning (think of Smokey Mountain in the Philippines), and the worms, which were hard to exterminate, kept coming back.

This imagery, then, does not have to mean that people cast into

Gehenna are tormented for ever. It could mean being finally destroyed: the 'annihilation' theory that many biblical scholars believe.

Notice, too, in Matthew, that it's 'the heirs of the kingdom' who are thrown into the darkness, while 'many from east and west' are welcomed. God's choice of who goes to life and who to destruction may not be the same as ours. Our calling is to 'work out [our] own salvation with fear and trembling' (Philippians 2:12), sacrificing everything that hinders our progress.

REFLECTION

Should we speak less of God's anger at sin, and more of the love God has shown us in Christ?

110

AN EMPTY HELL?

1 PETER 3:18–20a; 4:6

For Christ also suffered for sins once for all, the righteous for the unrighteous, in order to bring you to God. He was put to death in the flesh, but made alive in the spirit, in which also he went and made a proclamation to the spirits in prison, who in former times did not obey...

For this is the reason the gospel was proclaimed even to the dead, so that, though they had been judged in the flesh as everyone is judged, they might live in the spirit as God does.

Imagine you have fallen into a deep pit and injured yourself so badly that you can't climb out. Two rescuers arrive. One says, 'Here, I've got a rope ladder; I'll drop it and you climb up.' The other says, 'I'm coming down with a ladder and I'll carry you up.' Which would you choose?

These strange verses from Peter concern an idea that early theologians developed as 'the harrowing of hell'. You may have seen Orthodox icons in which Christ reaches out his hand to help up the 'imprisoned spirits'.

The thought behind it is that there can be nowhere in the universe, physical or spiritual, into which Christ's crucified love has not reached. Peter defines the 'spirits who did not obey' as those who were drowned when they refused to enter Noah's ark. It is a fitting image for those who, perhaps through ignorance, have failed to follow the call of Christ when they heard it. It might even encompass those who have never heard.

I like this teaching (and so do some scholars). I've long felt that if there is no chance of redemption after death, then God's purpose is defeated by death—which is exactly what the resurrection says it isn't.

So another alternative way of thinking is that hell may, eventually, be empty of all except those who choose to remain there—and even for them, eternity may offer a rescue plan. Hell, in this case, would 'at the last' be destroyed. For those who've been through a few hells on earth, that's quite a promise.

REFLECTION

'For he must reign until he has put all his enemies under his feet. The last enemy to be destroyed is death' (1 Corinthians 15:25–26). Let these verses stay in your mind today.

111

UNDEFEATABLE

MATTHEW 16:15–18

He said to them, 'But who do you say that I am?' Simon Peter answered, 'You are the Messiah, the Son of the living God.' And Jesus answered him, 'Blessed are you, Simon son of Jonah! For flesh and blood has not revealed this to you, but my Father in heaven. And I tell you, you are Peter, and on this rock I will build my church, and the gates of Hades will not prevail against it.'

As I drive my son to school, I've been passing every day a site where an old house has been demolished. A new, very nice (and probably very expensive) house is slowly being built. But for months, nothing seemed to be happening except preparing the ground and putting in foundations.

As a carpenter, Jesus probably knew a fair bit about house construction. He knew, for instance, that a good foundation is the key: rock is great; sand is a bad idea. So he founded his church—which is the advance guard of God's kingdom—on a rock. That rock was not just Peter the individual (who could be decidedly 'rocky' in another sense), but Peter's insight into who Jesus is and what he means.

Many Christians worry about whether God really accepts them, or whether they have committed 'the unforgivable sin' (see Matthew 12:31–32). Could I be one of those 'whitewashed tombs' (23:27) who looks godly but inside is full of rubbish? (Yes, actually, but God's doing a clearout job.) Might I be destined for hell? Or could I be inadvertently possessed by a demon?

Jesus' words to Peter assure us that his body, the church, is stronger than it may look. If we are 'in Christ', nothing, not even hell itself, can stand up to us. We are safe.

The image used here is of a walled and gated city under siege by an invading army. To batter down a fortified gate, you need a whole group of people to hold the battering ram. We need to be in this spiritual battle together. That doesn't mean we all need to think the same, believe the same, do the same—just that we love and support each other.

REFLECTION

'Do not fear those who kill the body but cannot kill the soul; rather fear him who can destroy both soul and body in hell' (Matthew 10:28).

112

HIDDEN HEAVEN

MATTHEW 4:17; 13:31–33

From that time Jesus began to proclaim, 'Repent, for the kingdom of heaven has come near.' ...

He put before them another parable: 'The kingdom of heaven is like a mustard seed that someone took and sowed in his field; it is the smallest of all the seeds, but when it has grown it is the greatest of shrubs and becomes a tree, so that the birds of the air come and make nests in its branches.'

He told them another parable: 'The kingdom of heaven is like yeast that a woman took and mixed in with three measures of flour until all of it was leavened.'

Before our son was born, Ed and I used to bake all our own bread (life was easier then). Now I only do so for special occasions. Recently I got out my 'long life' yeast and made up a batch of dough. After an hour in a cool oven, it still hadn't risen. My yeast had been in the cupboard so long that it was 'life expired'.

'The kingdom of heaven' is a phrase that only occurs in Matthew, the most Jewish of the Gospels. Jews were not allowed to say the name of God (Yahweh), so Matthew found an alternative. The parallel phrase in other Gospels is 'the kingdom of God'.

Jesus portrays this kingdom as something that starts small, like a little piece of yeast or a tiny seed. It is hidden among the dough or in the earth—no one notices it. Yet it will grow into food for many, or a home for all the birds.

This teaching is not about some far-off region beyond death. In Jesus, heaven has come near; we can step right into its borderlands. Jews of that time believed in seven heavens, each enclosed in the next, and the first was the air around us. So when we pray, 'Our Father in heaven', we could think, 'Our Father who is as close as the air we breathe.'

When we follow Jesus, we find yeast that never reaches the end of its life.

REFLECTION

'Not in the dark of buildings confining, not in some heaven light years away, but here in this place, the new light is shining; now is the kingdom, now is the day' (*Marty Haugen*, Mennonite Hymnal, *1992*)

113

MORE TO LIFE

LUKE 18:29–30; JOHN 5:24

And he said to them, 'Truly I tell you, there is no one who has left house or wife or brothers or parents or children, for the sake of the kingdom of God, who will not get back very much more in this age, and in the age to come eternal life.'

'Very truly, I tell you, anyone who hears my word and believes him who sent me has eternal life, and does not come under judgment, but has passed from death to life.'

In Douglas Adams' hit radio series and book *The Hitchhiker's Guide to the Galaxy*, robot servants have personality to make them more 'human'. One such is 'Marvin the paranoid android', a permanently depressed character who mutters, 'Life? Don't talk to me about life!'

Jesus does, however, talk about life—much more than he talks about heaven. To a Samaritan woman at a well, he promises 'a spring of water gushing up to eternal life' (John 4:14). To the disciples, he promises that whatever sacrifices—material, social, emotional—they have made to follow him, they will be rewarded even in this life. To those who believe what he says about God (which shows in what they do), he says that they are already on the other side of death, living a whole new quality of life. Paul links this to baptism, saying that we are 'buried with him in baptism' and 'raised with him through faith' (Colossians 2:12). I still remember that feeling of 'Now I have started a new life' as I came up out of the water.

Eternal life starts in the ordinary, not very exciting, sometimes very wearing lives we lead today. Jesus speaks of salvation in the same way. As Zacchaeus promises to pay back his victims and give half his criminal earnings to the poor, Jesus exclaims, 'Today salvation has come to this house' (Luke 19:8–9).

There may be times in your life when you feel 'half alive' (or half dead!). Nevertheless, Paul says, although in our struggles we are 'always carrying in the body the death of Jesus', it is 'so that the life of Jesus may also be made visible in our bodies' (2 Corinthians 4:10).

REFLECTION

'Do not work for the food that perishes, but for the food that endures for eternal life' (John 6:27).

114

END OF THE BEGINNING

1 CORINTHIANS 15:19–24

If for this life only we have hoped in Christ, we are of all people most to be pitied.

But in fact Christ has been raised from the dead, the first fruits of those who have died. For since death came through a human being, the resurrection of the dead has also come through a human being; for as all die in Adam, so all will be made alive in Christ. But each in his own order: Christ the first fruits, then at his coming those who belong to Christ. Then comes the end, when he hands over the kingdom to God the Father, after he has destroyed every ruler and every authority and power.

When I hear people say, 'Charity begins at home', I always want to ask, 'But need it end there?'

Eternal life begins now, but if it ends there, our hope isn't very great. Christians, just like others, go through poverty, illness and breakdown of relationships. But 'hope does not disappoint us, because God's love has been poured into our hearts through the Holy Spirit' (Romans 5:5). That Holy Spirit in us is a 'first instalment' of our heavenly heritage (2 Corinthians 1:22), a 'seal for the day of redemption' (Ephesians 4:30). Our hope is for the present and the future (and even the past, as God by his Spirit heals past hurts).

More than that: our hope is not merely an individual one, in which God saves people 'like a brand plucked from the fire' (Zechariah 3:2, a favourite verse of John Wesley, who was rescued from a house fire as a child). Even this verse actually refers to all of God's people; and in today's reading we have an extraordinary promise—that 'all will be made alive in Christ'. Some take this to mean that all people will eventually recognize Christ and live. It is certainly a picture of a far-reaching redemption, in which all powers that defy God will eventually be destroyed.

REFLECTION

After a great Allied victory in World War II, Churchill said, 'This is not the end. It is not even the beginning of the end; but it is, perhaps, the end of the beginning.' We could say something similar of our hope in Christ.

115

ONLY JESUS

LUKE 23:39–43

One of the criminals who were hanged there kept deriding him and saying, 'Are you not the Messiah? Save yourself and us!' But the other rebuked him, saying, 'Do you not fear God, since you are under the same sentence of condemnation? And we indeed have been condemned justly, for we are getting what we deserve for our deeds, but this man has done nothing wrong.' Then he said, 'Jesus, remember me when you come into your kingdom.' He replied, 'Truly I tell you, today you will be with me in Paradise.'

Ed and I had just arrived back from a weekend trip to Brussels. One thing I had put carefully in a safe place was our airport car park ticket. That was our means of getting home.

I'm not keen on 'ticket to heaven' images of faith. They can imply that as long as we've signed on the dotted line of some confession of faith, nothing else need happen. God looks for godly actions as evidence of our faith—just as our local education authority is asking that I bring to the special needs tribunal some evidence of my faith that our son needs a statement of special needs.

This condemned burglar, however, has no history of love to take with him to the cross—nothing except his recognition that, in Jesus, a new kingdom has arrived, a kingdom not defeated even by death. Yet Jesus, without hesitation, promises him paradise, and more—to be 'with me'.

We may be judged by our actions but we are not saved by them. God will examine how we have built on the foundation of Jesus— 'with gold, silver, precious stones, wood, hay, straw' (1 Corinthians 3:12)—and 'if what has been built on the foundation survives, the builder will receive a reward' (v. 14). Nevertheless, even though our good works are few and feeble, if we belong to Jesus we will still be saved (v. 15). Ultimately, we need nothing but a love of Jesus and a desire to follow him wherever he goes. And where he's going is to a new world of which we can be a part.

PRAYER

'It is correct to say "God is love"; it is wrong to say "God is wrath"' (Randy Klassen). Praise God for the mercy you have received.

116

BEING AGNOSTIC

1 CORINTHIANS 15:35–38, 51–53

But someone will ask, 'How are the dead raised? With what kind of body do they come?' Fool! What you sow does not come to life unless it dies. And as for what you sow, you do not sow the body that is to be, but a bare seed, perhaps of wheat or of some other grain. But God gives it a body as he has chosen, and to each kind of seed its own body...

Listen, I will tell you a mystery! We will not all die, but we will all be changed, in a moment, in the twinkling of an eye, at the last trumpet. For the trumpet will sound, and the dead will be raised imperishable, and we will be changed. For this perishable body must put on imperishability, and this mortal body must put on immortality.

My son's teacher has brought into the classroom a butterfly hatchery. Each little Perspex pot contains a caterpillar and all the food it will need until it spins its cocoon. If you could ask the caterpillar what will happen when it comes out of that cocoon, I'm sure it would have no idea. No butterfly has ever come back to tell it about flying!

On Ascension Day, we remember the risen Jesus returning to God and no longer being visible to his disciples. Where is Jesus now? What does it mean that he who was human is part of the God's very being, the Trinity?

When Ed and I travel together by car, the driver generally lets the passenger navigate. To go on a journey into the unknown, you only need to trust your guide. Jesus trusted his Father; we can trust Jesus. We don't need to know more.

One thing we can know about the new heaven and new earth is that, in some way, it will resemble the universe we now inhabit. Paul talks in terms of a risen body—something that can sense, feed, love.

Last night, I saw on television a woman who, through a rare virus, had lost all sense of touch. Not feeling the ground, she couldn't walk, and every daily task was a feat of hand-eye co-ordination. She was effectively 'disembodied'. Heaven will not be like that.

PRAYER

Jesus, give me all the spiritual food I need to grow my wings.

117

NOT OUR JOB

MATTHEW 13:24–30 (ABRIDGED)

He put before them another parable: 'The kingdom of heaven may be compared to someone who sowed good seed in his field; but while everybody was asleep, an enemy came and sowed weeds among the wheat, and then went away. So when the plants came up and bore grain, then the weeds appeared as well... The slaves said to [their master], "Then do you want us to go and gather them?" But he replied, "No; for in gathering the weeds you would uproot the wheat along with them. Let both of them grow together until the harvest; and at harvest time I will tell the reapers, Collect the weeds first and bind them in bundles to be burned, but gather the wheat into my barn."'

A friend at church is offering everyone a self-set ash tree from his garden. No one has taken up the offer; they have enough uninvited ash and sycamore saplings in their own gardens.

We may disagree as to whether weeds are an invention of Satan. (I've always rather liked bindweed flowers—but not on my roses!) The real problem of the weeds is that until everything is fully grown, you cannot tell green field grass from green wheat.

Remember that the whole field here belongs to the farmer, just as the whole world belongs to God. There will be inedible, uninvited grass in God's wheat field, but we are not the ones appointed to tell the difference. We might be so zealous in pulling up weeds that we destroy some perfectly good wheat. (Does that sound at all like any incidents in church history?)

Roger Wagner's stunning painting *The Harvest Is the End of the World, and the Reapers are Angels* (1984) shows a ripe cornfield with powerful winged figures setting their sickles to the stalks of the grain. There is a harvest; but we are not the reapers.

REFLECTION

'But woe to you, scribes and Pharisees, hypocrites! For you lock people out of the kingdom of heaven. For you do not go in yourselves, and when others are going in, you stop them… For you cross sea and land to make a single convert, and you make the new convert twice as much a child of hell as yourselves' (Matthew 23:13–15). *Let us not lock the door too hastily.*

118

FREE AT LAST

REVELATION 20:14—21:5 (ABRIDGED)

Then Death and Hades were thrown into the lake of fire. This is the second death, the lake of fire; and anyone whose name was not found written in the book of life was thrown into the lake of fire.

Then I saw a new heaven and a new earth; for the first heaven and the first earth had passed away... And I saw the holy city, the new Jerusalem, coming down out of heaven from God, prepared as a bride adorned for her husband... And the one who was seated on the throne said, 'See, I am making all things new.'

Why a new heaven as well as a new earth? What was wrong with the old one? 'Heaven' in the Bible can mean just 'sky', so this could simply mean 'a whole new universe'. However, 'heaven' can also mean 'God's realm'. This passage may be saying that heaven is not created yet—that it will be ushered in at the end of time. Immortality of the soul—the spirit living on separately from the dead body—is an idea from Greek philosophy. The Bible's teaching, by contrast, majors on the resurrection of the body 'on the last day'.

Of course, as Tony Campolo points out, God is outside time, so when that day comes, the distinction between 'now' and 'in the future' will be meaningless. The kingdom of God (which Jesus talked about far more than heaven) is both now and to come. Then, death will be among the things that have 'passed away'. Now, death is still among us, but it is defeated.

The important thing for us now is to live, by God's Spirit, as if the kingdom is already here. Jesus gave Peter 'the keys of the kingdom of heaven' and said, 'Whatever you bind on earth will be bound in heaven, and whatever you loose on earth will be loosed in heaven' (Matthew 16:19). We are God's heavenly delegates, and our actions of imprisoning or freeing have eternal consequences. We should major on freeing people, and imprisoning only the forces of evil.

REFLECTION

'Do not be afraid; I am the first and the last, and the living one. I was dead, and see, I am alive for ever and ever; and I have the keys of Death and of Hades' (Revelation 1:17–18).

✣

THE DISAPPOINTMENT

From some people's idea of heaven, I'm not at all sure I want to go there!
One preacher declared, 'Don't think that heaven is a rest. You'll have to work
really hard at praising God all the time.' I don't know where he got this
extremely unbiblical idea. Anyway, in this column, I was inspired to respond
to what I saw as a very unimaginative view of what God might have in store
for us.

As soon as they heard the unearthly, unmistakable sound, they knew
it was the day they had been waiting for. It didn't seem to take any
time at all for them to get there—if 'getting there' was the right way
to put it, for time and distance no longer meant anything. They felt
extraordinarily fresh, as though they had just been awakened from a
very long sleep. They could hardly contain their anticipation. They
began to explore.

It was then that they became puzzled. There could hardly be
any mistake, but everything was so different from what they had
expected. If they hadn't known better, they would almost have said
that it was only a pale and thin imitation of what they had known
before. They surely couldn't be… it wasn't… but no, there was no
doubt that they were in the right place. It just wasn't quite how they
had envisaged it.

There were the buildings, for a start. They appeared very plain,
somewhat shoddy and—well, ugly. There were the odd bits of
decoration, it was true, but they were tacked on as if in afterthought,
and the overall proportions weren't particularly pleasing. In fact, the
general impression could only be called forbidding. What was more,
the style didn't seem to belong to any particular period, but was a
sort of amalgam of all known historical fashions. This was to be

expected, they supposed, if the idea was to convey timelessness; but they *had* rather hoped for something nobler.

Then there was the landscape in which the buildings stood. That at least had a certain beauty, but they couldn't help feeling it showed an artificial, manufactured quality. It reminded them of nothing so much as the tops of old-fashioned chocolate boxes, and the idea was reinforced by the writing all over the mountains. It really did get in the way of their appreciation. In addition, there was an all-pervading smell which seemed to be rising from the ground—not an invigorating smell like pine forests or sea air, but something more like a suffocating blend of school floor polish, disinfectant, gravy powder and boiling marmalade. 'The odour of sanctity' was a phrase that, unbidden, leapt into the mind of one of the group, while another began to wonder whether, contrary to everything he had thought before, incense wasn't so bad after all.

Perhaps most disturbing of all was the music playing in the background. The lyrics were undoubtedly laudable, since they dealt with matters that the whole group agreed to be important; but it had to be admitted that they were rather repetitive, and not exactly what one would want to hear for ever. They showed a painful lack of any real depth or originality, and much of the grammar wasn't very good, while the verses often didn't scan and some of the rhymes were, frankly, appalling. Coupled with the slushiness of the tunes, the effect was—if we are to be truthful—one of cheap and even irritating sentimentality.

Finally, the new arrivals took a good look at themselves and each other. Here at least they had anticipated seeing real glory and splendour—something beyond anything they had ever experienced before. This was the moment of greatest disappointment. Their clothes were plain, ill-fitting, badly made and extremely unflattering. The best that could be said for the garments was that they might be practical for doing dirty jobs—if there was such a thing to be done here. As for their facial expressions—well, some looked as though they had never had a moment's enjoyment in their lives, while others were fixed in an inane grin which was perhaps supposed to be benevolent, but which no one in their right mind would want to look at for very long. Taken all in all, it was soon clear that they didn't like themselves or each other very much.

The questions weren't long in coming. What is this? Is this all there is? Were our visions mistaken? Or will it get better? Have we got it wrong? Are we not chosen after all? Have you rejected us?

Unearthly, unmistakable, the voice pierced the hubbub. 'No,' it said, 'you are not in the wrong place. I have done all I could for you. Everyone gets what they choose, and this is what you chose. You are right, it is not as good as what you had before. But you showed so little interest in the best of what I had given you there. You seemed positively to despise it at times. You even used the word "human" as a term of disapproval, so I thought you would prefer to become less so. You expended so much effort in producing the kind of thing you see here, and telling yourselves that it was really much better than what I had placed around you for your benefit. So I concluded that this was the sort of thing you liked. Here it is. You've got exactly what you wanted.'

After the voice had spoken, there was a deep silence, broken only by the already infuriating music. Then the group looked at each other and realized that the same thought was in all their minds. They would have to ask if they could go back, and try again.

BLIND SPOTS IN THE BIBLE

Puzzles and paradoxes that we tend to avoid

ADRIAN PLASS

'This book is filled with what I have called "blind spots" from the Bible. Some may be familiar passages, some more obscure, but what they have in common is at least one intriguing or disturbing aspect that I have previously missed, or noted out of the corner of my eye, but never got round to investigating or facing honestly. Why did Jesus weep at the tomb of Lazarus when he knew that his friend was about to be raised from the dead? What does the verse in Revelation mean about seeming alive when you are really dead, spiritually speaking? And what about the extraordinary bit in Genesis about angels marrying the beautiful daughters of men?

'There are, of course, many biblical stories and ideas that we will never fully understand until the day when God himself bestows the clarity that eludes us here. In the meantime, we are certainly allowed to think and analyse and question anything that strikes us as strange or inexplicable. I do hope you enjoy and benefit from my "blind spots" and I wish you a continuation of God's cheerful blessing as you investigate your own.'

ISBN 1 84101 505 9   £7.99
Available from your local Christian bookshop or, in case of difficulty, direct from BRF using the order form on page 301.

A YEAR WITH NEW DAYLIGHT

Daily readings from the Bible

ED. DAVID WINTER

This book brings together 366 readings from *New Daylight*, BRF's popular scheme of daily Bible readings. It provides a short reading, a helpful comment and a prayer or point of reflection for every day of the year, even in leap years! *New Daylight* is ideal for those looking for a fresh approach to regular Bible study. It reflects the changing patterns of the Christian calendar and a refreshing variety of style and approach from a talented team of contributors drawn from many different Christian traditions: Christine Chapman, Margaret Cundiff, Graham Dodds, Colin Evans, Rob Gillion, Peter Graves, Rosemary Green, Hilary McDowell, Marcus Maxwell, Adrian Plass, Brother Ramon SSF, Jenny Robertson, Henry Wansbrough OSB, David Winter and Veronica Zundel.

ISBN 1 84101 234 3 £12.99
Available from your local Christian bookshop or, in case of difficulty, direct from BRF using the order form on page 301.

SPIRITED WOMEN

Encountering the first women believers

MARY ELLEN ASHCROFT

Spirited Women is an invitation to travel across time and space in order to encounter lost relatives in the Christian faith. Set during the time of the book of Acts, just after the death of Stephen, the first martyr, it explores the stories of some of the women involved in the early Church—Mary Magdalene, Martha, Mary the mother of Jesus, and Joanna, among others.

Drawing on the author's theological and historical research, biblical study and imagination, this book brings vivid life to women who have been largely forgotten or marginalized over the years. Exploring their experiences and their resilient faith, we too can be challenged and empowered in our walk with God. *Spirited Women* also includes questions that can be used for group or individual study, notes for further reading, and a detailed bibliography.

ISBN 1 84101 443 5   £6.99
Available from your local Christian bookshop or, in case of difficulty, direct from BRF using the order form on page 301.

GOD HAS DAUGHTERS TOO

ABIDEMI SANUSI

Ten women. Ten stories. One God.
Eve • Sarah • Leah • Zipporah • Deborah • Michal • Bathsheba
Esther • Job's wife • Gomer

Hear the lives of these Bible women as you've never heard them before: their individual battles with family tensions, powerlessness, love and loss—and their relationship with the God of love, who will not let them go, no matter how many times they kick against him. While these ten women lived in exceptional times, the issues and choices they faced are not so different from those we face today. And just as they experienced God's grace, so we can experience it at work in our circumstances, no matter how difficult.

ISBN 1 84101 417 6   £6.99
Available from your local Christian bookshop or, in case of difficulty, direct from BRF using the order form on page 301.

ORDER FORM

REF	TITLE	PRICE	QTY	TOTAL
505 9	*Blind Spots in the Bible*	£7.99		
234 3	*A Year with New Daylight*	£12.99		
443 5	*Spirited Women*	£6.99		
417 6	*God Has Daughters Too*	£6.99		

POSTAGE AND PACKING CHARGES						
Order value	UK	Europe	Surface	Air Mail	Postage and packing:	
£7.00 & under	£1.25	£3.00	£3.50	£5.50	Donation:	
£7.01–£30.00	£2.25	£5.50	£6.50	£10.00	Total enclosed:	
Over £30.00	free	prices on request				

Name _____ Account Number _____

Address _____

_____ Postcode _____

Telephone Number _____ Email _____

Payment by: ❏ Cheque ❏ Mastercard ❏ Visa ❏ Postal Order ❏ Switch

Card no. ❏❏❏❏ ❏❏❏❏ ❏❏❏❏ ❏❏❏❏

Expires ❏❏ ❏❏   Issue no. of Switch card ❏❏❏

Signature _____ Date _____

All orders must be accompanied by the appropriate payment.

Please send your completed order form to:
BRF, First Floor, Elsfield Hall, 15–17 Elsfield Way, Oxford OX2 8FG
Tel. 01865 319700 / Fax. 01865 319701 Email: enquiries@brf.org.uk

❏ Please send me further information about BRF publications.

Available from your local Christian bookshop.   BRF is a Registered Charity